英语时文泛读 (第1册)

Current News Articles for Extensive Reading

总主编　范守义
主　编　石　毅　于　倩

北京大学出版社
PEKING UNIVERSITY PRESS

图书在版编目(CIP)数据

英语时文泛读(第1册)/石毅,于倩主编. —北京：北京大学出版社,2009.1
(21世纪英语专业系列教材)
ISBN 978-7-301-14495-4

Ⅰ.英… Ⅱ.①石…②于… Ⅲ.英语－阅读教学－高等学校－教材 Ⅳ.H319.4

中国版本图书馆CIP数据核字(2008)第176927号

书　　　名：英语时文泛读(第1册)
著作责任者：石　毅　于　倩　主编
责 任 编 辑：汪晓丹
标 准 书 号：ISBN 978-7-301-14495-4/H·2132
出 版 发 行：北京大学出版社
地　　　址：北京市海淀区成府路205号　100871
网　　　址：http://www.pup.cn
编辑部邮箱：pupwaiwen@pup.cn
总编室邮箱：zpup@pup.cn
电　　　话：邮购部 62752015　发行部 62750672　编辑部 62759634　出版部 62756370
印　刷　者：北京飞达印刷有限责任公司
经　销　者：新华书店
　　　　　　787毫米×1092毫米　16开本　8.75印张　220千字
　　　　　　2009年1月第1版　2023年8月第9次印刷
定　　　价：36.00元

未经许可,不得以任何方式复制或抄袭本书之部分或全部内容。
版权所有,侵权必究
举报电话：(010)62752024　电子信箱：fd@pup.pku.edu.cn

写给本书使用者的话

21世纪的中国是改革向广度和深度进军的世纪，21世纪的世界是全球化走向优化整合和更高水平的世纪。中国与世界各国交往向全方位推进和巩固是历史发展之必然。走在历史发展最前沿的是双语或多语工作者；而在当今的世界上，英语使用之广泛是举世公认的。中国的外语教育中英语是最为重要的外国语言。外交学院作为外语类院校在过去的半个多世纪中为中国外交外事和各个部门培养了大批外语人才，他们在各个领域发挥了巨大作用，做出了杰出的贡献。

外交学院是具有外交特色和外语优势的重点大学，外交学院的英语教学在复校后的三十年中，积累了丰富的教学经验。英语时文泛读是外交学院英语本科教学的核心课程；该课程为学生提高英语阅读水平，扩大词汇量和阅读技巧，丰富文化和国际知识提供了很好的学习平台。学习这门课程以及其他相关课程，可为学生走向职场奠定坚实的基础。外交学院培养出的学生具有国际视野和外交外事专业水准是十分恰当的评价。

2005年以来外交学院英语系将英语泛读作为精品项目立项，2007年夏被评为北京市精品课程。目前我们正在向国家级精品课程努力。该精品课程由两大板块组成，即课堂教学和课外阅读——课堂教学使用了精选的时文作为主要的教学内容；课外阅读使用了精选的英语简易读物、注释读物和英语原著作为主要内容，并为每一部书设计了一百个问题，可以在计算机网络上进行在线测试，并立即得到结果，同时教师也能够立即看到全部参加测试者的成绩以及学生学期和学年的累计成绩。我们与北京外国语大学英语学院和首都师范大学外国语学院英语系合作，进行异地登录测试也取得了满意的结果。这种英语泛读课程创新的教学模式为迅速提高学生的英语水平和综合运用能力起到了很好的作用，深受教师和学生的欢迎。

这里我们主要谈一下课堂用书《英语时文泛读》的编辑情况。

我们的编辑设计思路如下：

1. 所选文本要语言地道，内容新颖（除个别为略早的文章，其余课文全部为2005年以后英美主要报刊杂志上发表的文章），题材广泛多样（涉及政治、经济、文化、教育、科技、环保、法律、社会等诸方面内容），贴近时代与生活，易激发学生兴趣。
2. 该教材就不同主题设不同单元，知识内容较成体系，既有助于学生系统学习、积累和运用所学知识，又有助于学生分类学习记忆相关词汇。

3. 练习设计合理、实用，既有很强的针对性（针对每个单元具体的阅读技巧及目标），又能考察学生的综合能力，形式比较灵活，易于操作。

4. 为使所选用的文本难度符合学生的英语程度，既不要过易，也不要过难，我们使用了根据美国著名教育家鲁道夫·弗莱施(Rudolf Flesch)博士的"英语文章难易度与单位长度的音节数和词数密切相关"理论，将数学模型化，并在其基础上编写的程序，进行《英语时文泛读》文本的选材，剔除了过难和过易的文本。

5. 编写旨在为使用《英语时文泛读》的教师准备的《教师参考书》，提供必要而丰富的备课参考资料和练习答案。

6. 制作课堂使用的PPT文档，供授课使用，教师亦可增添或删节内容，以适应具体需要。

7. 编辑快速阅读文本，以及相关的英国英语和美国英语的知识等内容，供教学参考使用。

8. 使用者可以根据本教学单位学生的英语水平，使用合适的单元和文本长度进行课堂阅读活动。

9. 为了锻炼学生自己查字典和确定词义的能力，在文本A和文本B之后的词汇表中，只给出没有在练习中出现的词；为照顾部分学生学习的需要，各单元的生词按英语字母表列在全书之后，学生可以查阅、记忆，然后再去做练习。

10. 在使用本教材时，教师应特别注意有些单元中有关中国国情的文本内容的真实性，由于外国记者的立场、观点与我们的不同，对事实的调查和资料的把握也不一定准确，所以其陈述很可能有不实之处。使用者应根据实际情况，在授课时作适当更正。

为保证教材编写的专业水准，我们组成了以范守义教授为负责人的《英语时文泛读》教程编辑委员会，人员如下：

范守义：总主编，负责策划统筹、审阅和编辑等工作。

石毅、于倩：共同主编，负责《英语时文泛读》第一册的编写工作；

张蕾、吴晓萍：共同主编，负责《英语时文泛读》第二册的编写工作；

武波、王振玲：共同主编，负责《英语时文泛读》第三册的编写工作；

徐英、魏腊梅：共同主编，负责《英语时文泛读》第四册的编写工作。

我们期待《英语时文泛读》的出版能够为我国大学本科和程度相当的英语学习者提供一套新的泛读教程，以满足与时俱进的教学要求；为此我们期待广大教师和学生提出宝贵意见和要求，以改进我们的编辑工作。我们也期待以《英语时文泛读》为主和能进行在线测试的课外阅读为辅的创新英语泛读教学模式为推动和提升全国泛读教学做出贡献。

《英语时文泛读》教程编辑委员会
2008年9月26日

目 录
CONTENTS

UNIT ONE　EDUCATION　　1

　　Text A　Battling the One Bad Apple　/　1

　　Text B　Which College Brings the Bling　/　6

　　Text C　Mixed Results on Paying City Students to Pass Tests　/　10

UNIT TWO　ENVIRONMENTAL PROTECTION　　15

　　Text A　New Orleans Disaster Serves Up a Tough Lesson on Environment　/　15

　　Text B　Forest Loss in Sumatra Becomes a Global Issue　/　21

　　Text C　Nine States in Plan to Cut Emissions by Power Plant　/　27

UNIT THREE　CHINA HORIZONS　　32

　　Text A　Numbers Game in China　/　32

　　Text B　New Wealth Buys Makeovers in China　/　38

　　Text C　New Struggle in China: Keep Up with the Chans　/　45

UNIT FOUR　GREAT BRITAIN TODAY　　48

　　Text A　Is Britain Still Home of Mannerly Charm? Don't be Daft!　/　48

　　Text B　Saving the Day　/　54

　　Text C　Come and Fall on Slough　/　58

UNIT FIVE THE CHANGING AMERICAN CULTURE 61

Text A Demand Growing for Taller Christmas Trees / 61

Text B Storm Changed Americans' Attitudes / 66

Text C How to Tell if You're American? / 71

UNIT SIX COMMUNICATION AND INTERPERSONAL SKILLS 77

Text A Maintain a Healthy Relationship with Your Parents / 77

Text B How to Mend a Broken Friendship: Reach Out to Old Friends / 84

Text C Is Your Marriage in Trouble? / 89

UNIT SEVEN CAMPUS LIFE IN THE USA 93

Text A There's More to College Life Than Classes: Get Involved! / 93

Text B College Survival Tips for the Nontraditional College Students'
         Successful Entry to College Life and a College Education / 99

Text C Commencement Address at Wellesley College / 104

UNIT EIGHT LAW IN EVERYDAY LIFE 108

Text A You're Being Duped / 108

Text B Get' Em Off the Road! / 114

Text C Expel These Teachers / 119

GLOSSARY / *123*

UNIT ONE

EDUCATION

Target of the Unit

☞ To get a glimpse of modern education of the US
☞ To practice reading skills
☞ To enlarge your vocabulary

1) LEAD IN

Directions: In this unit, you will read 3 passages about education. Read them and think about the purpose of education.

2) DISCUSSION

In your opinion, what role should education play in the growth of a person?

Text A

Battling the One Bad Apple

By Eric L. Wee

Warming-up Exercises

☞ What do you think should be the normal relationship between the teacher and the students? What should we do to bring teachers and students closer together?

· First reading ·

Directions: Now please read the following passage as fast as you can and summarize the main idea.

1

1 I hated him. I didn't plan on it. In fact, I wanted to like S. I wanted him to like me.

2 Before teaching my first college journalism class at a private university in Virginia, I expected to forge friendships with all my students. I'd be that young cool professor, **approachable** and informal. I'd have my students call me Eric. We'd laugh and hang out. And they'd love my class.

> **approachable** *adj.* friendly and easy to talk to 平易近人的
> **nemesis** *n.* an opponent that cannot be beaten or overcome 难以取胜的对手，劲敌，死对头
> **downer** *n.* one that depresses, such as an experience or person 使沮丧的事或不争气的人
> **vibes** *n.* the good or bad feelings that a particular person, place, or situation seems to produce and that you react to 气氛，环境

3 Then the first day of the semester arrived, and there it was—this invisible line I wasn't sure how to cross. The students were on one side of it. And I was on the other. I tried to chat with a few of them, but it felt forced and awkward. I had this unnerving feeling that I was a stand-up comedian hoping to win their applause. In the corner, S. looked as if he was about to fall asleep.

4 Each week, I would try new things to engage the students and make the class fun. I created mock news conferences. I took them on a walking tour and had them write about it on deadline. But S. rolled his eyes with each new project. One day I asked the class to write about an important person in their lives, an assignment designed to hone their use of details. S. let out a sigh that echoed across the room.

5 He became my **nemesis**. The night before class, I'd lie in bed thinking about how I had to endure him the next day. I could see his moppish hair dangling over his eyes, his slouch, his bored look. I dreaded him. Yet somehow I still thought I'd win him over. Instead, as the weeks rolled by, things got worse. S.'s disdain for the class and for me grew more open. He was a virus, and he was contaminating everyone around him! A lesson would be flowing, the students enthusiastic, and S. would bring it to a halt with his **downer vibes**.

6 One day in class, I met with the students individually to talk about their projects. The others waited for their turn. But S. grew impatient and started to walk out before I caught him and asked him to sit. He did so reluctantly. His e-mails to me began to get ruder.

7 Finally I'd had enough. I called him to my office and told him I wanted him out of the class. I had no other choice. He was infecting the other students with

his derision, I explained. Surprisingly, he seemed to understand. He didn't argue or get belligerent. Instead, he nodded and left.

> **boot** *n.* (*slang*) an unceremonious dismissal, as from a job, used with the boot 撵走
> **buddy** *n.* a good friend; a comrade 好友，哥们

8   After he dropped the course, I felt terrible. And terrific. I wasn't making friends with my students; I was giving them the **boot**! Yet I knew this had been the right thing to do. S. had forced me to take back control of my class. And in the process, he'd taught me something valuable: Sometimes, you need to be tough to be a good teacher. My fantasies about college teaching had been naïve. My students and I weren't going to be **buddies**. But I could create and maintain an environment where they could learn.

9   I ran into S. months later on campus. I looked up and saw him heading my way. I wasn't sure what he'd say or do. Would he swear at me? Would he give me the finger? Instead as we got closer, he smiled. He was pleasant and asked how I was. We didn't talk about the class. Instead he just shook my hand. It was the nicest he'd ever been to me.

(Words: 609)

• Second Reading •

Directions: Read the text again more carefully to find enough information for Exercises I, II & III.

Exercise I   True or False

Directions: Please state whether the following statements are true or false (T/F) according to what you've found in the text.

1. The author was quite optimistic about his future career at the very beginning.
2. He would like to become a very formal and strict professor who can help the students learn in college.
3. S. became the obstacle the first day he started his teaching.
4. The author tried his best to make the classroom as active as possible by introducing various kinds of activities.
5. Although S. did not want to do the homework and tended to fall asleep in class, the other students were not influenced by him.

6. S.'s attitude toward the author was getting more and more negative after the author drove him out of class.

7. S. was quite calm when the author asked him to leave the class.

8. Finally the author realized that his dream about the teaching career had been too naïve.

9. The author learned how to relate to the students from his experience with S.

10. The encounter between the author and S was quite hostile after S. dropped the course.

> **Exercise II Word Inference**
>
> *Directions: Often you can guess the meaning of a word/expression by reading the words around it. Please read the given sentence to see how each word/expression in bold type is used in the text. Then choose the answer that is closest in meaning to the bold-faced word/expression.*

1. Before teaching my first college journalism class at a private university in Virginia, I expected to **forge** friendships with all my students.

   A. beat

   B. build

   C. recreate

   D. counterfeit

2. I'd be that young **cool** professor, approachable and informal.

   A. cold   B. calm

   C. uninterested   D. pleasant

3. I had this **unnerving** feeling that I was a stand-up comedian hoping to win their applause.

   A. discouraging

   B. embarrassing

   C. disgusting

   D. humiliating

4. One day I asked the class to write about an important person in their lives, an assignment designed to **hone** their use of details.

   A. sharpen

   B. desire

   C. demand

   D. facilitate

5. I could see his moppish hair dangling over his eyes, his **slouch**, his bored look.

   A. laziness

   B. muteness

   C. rudeness

   D. restlessness

6. S.'s **disdain** for the class and for me grew more open.

   A. reluctance   B. dislike

   C. disposal   D. displeasure

7. A lesson would be **flowing**, the students enthusiastic, and S. would bring it to a halt with his downer vibes.

   A. continuing in a smooth, graceful way

   B. continuing in a smooth, uncontrolled way

   C. continuing in a noisy, uncontrolled way

   D. continuing in a free, uncontrolled way

8. He was infecting the other students with his **derision**, I explained.

   A. erosion   B. tardiness

   C. mockery   D. restlessness

9. He didn't argue or get **belligerent**. Instead, he nodded and left.

   A. aggressive   B. annoyed

   C. excited   D. rude

10. Sometimes, you need to be **tough** to be a good teacher.

    A. violent

    B. unyielding

    C. difficult

    D. unfortunate

Exercise III Discussion

Directions: Please discuss the following questions in pairs or groups.

1. Imagine that you are the teacher in that classroom. What measures will you take to battle the one bad apple in the classroom? Work out your proposed action plan, and be prepared to present it to the class.

Text B

Which College Brings the Bling

By Devin Gordon and Joan Raymond

Warming-up Exercises

☞ How many kinds of recreation facilities does your university have? Which one do you like best, and why?

• First reading •

Directions: Now please read the following passage as fast as you can and summarize the main idea.

1 Once upon a time, a typical college freshman's day would begin something like this: wake up in a **creaky** dorm room, step over your roommate's dirty laundry, then step over your roommate, slump down the hall to the bathroom and brush your teeth next to a total stranger, hit the gym for a quick run, then stop off at the cafeteria before class for a nice breakfast of **runny** eggs. It wasn't glamorous, but that was OK, because you were there for your *education*. And now? Put it this way: colleges no longer use icky words like dorm or cafeteria. These days, you'll get a funny look unless you say residence hall, recreation center or dining marketplace.   __A__ . But it isn't just a pitch. All across the country, facilities devoted to students' extracurricular life are nicer than ever. A lot nicer. The lucky brats.

> **creaky** *adj.* something such as a door, floor, or bed that is creaky creaks when you open it, walk on it, sit on it etc, especially because it is old and not in good condition 吱嘎作响的
> **runny** *adj.* food that is runny is not as solid or thick as normal or as desired（食物因未熟或变质而变得）软，粘，稀溜溜的
> **best** *v.* to defeat someone 打败某人

2 It's no secret that the admissions process has become as ferocious as Tom Cruise in a roomful of psychiatrists, but it's not just the kids trying to **best** each other.   __B__ . The University of Houston's new rec facility features an outdoor pool with waterfalls, water slides and a hot tub that seats 20. The University of North Carolina at Chapel Hill just opened its $80 million Rams Head Center, complete with a 6,500-square-foot supermarket, a giant

food court with actual, edible food and a state-of-the-art sports bar with remotes at each table connected to a series of wall-mounted **plasma** TVs. Ohio State University's sparkling $140 million facility boasts massage rooms and saunas, plus an Adventure Recreation Center with a bouldering cave and 4,000 square feet of climbing wall, which should give jealous Mom and Dad something nice and high from which to hurl themselves.

> **plasma** *n.* It is a distinct phase of matter, separate from the traditional solids, liquids, and gases. It is a collection of charged particles that respond strongly and collectively to electromagnetic fields, taking the form of gas-like clouds or ion beams. Since the particles in plasma are electrically charged (generally by being stripped of electrons), it is frequently described as an "ionized gas." 此处指Digital High Definition Plasma TV 数字高清等离子电视
>
> **digs** *n.* lodging 宿舍

3   __C__. Jed Johnson, a recent Ohio State graduate, says the new rec center addressed a desperate need. "It was totally weird that a major university had these horrendous facilities," he says. The school's old gym was "a maze. You could die in the hallways and no one would ever find you." From a marketing perspective, Ohio State had to upgrade or risk losing students and athletic recruits to—hiss!—rival Michigan.

4   At the University of Missouri—Kansas City, the administration just put the finishing touches on its first new residence hall in nearly half a century, the $22 million, 561-bed Oak Street Hall, a suite-style building wired for the digitally savvy freshman. The building should ease grumbling that the school couldn't compete with neighboring universities for out-of-town students until it addressed its meager housing situation. Like most new residence halls, Oak Street is a welcome departure from the psych-ward look favored by dorms of the past. "My mom says I'm spoiled," says junior Matt Franklin. "I always hear, 'Back when I was in school...'" Of course, back when she was in school, a dorm room didn't cost $6,270 a year, which is what students pay to live large in Oak Street—$1,000 more than students pay for a similar room in a nearby hall.

5   ___D___. So where does the money come from? You. The schools borrow, then attach building-user fees to pay back the bonds. The downside is the risk of establishing class divisions on campus: the rich kids live in the fancy new **digs**. It's a risk, however, that colleges not only are willing to make but believe they must in order to compete.

> **largesse** n. (fml) when one gives money or gifts to people who have less than do, or the money or gifts that they give 慷慨大方

6   Some schools are even trying to woo students with, well, refreshments. On select Friday nights at Colby College, a private liberal-arts school in Maine, 21-and-older students can enjoy a nice South African Shiraz (and various microbrewed beers) served to them by a tuxedo-clad bartender. The wine tastings are part of Colby's alcohol-education efforts. For a dollar per varietal—cheaper than Schlit—undergrads get to drink the good stuff out of a crisp, clean wine glass. ___E___.

(Words: 757)

· Second Reading ·

Directions: Read the text again more carefully to find enough information for Exercises I, II, III, IV & V.

Exercise I   Understanding Text Organization

Directions: You may find there are a few sentences missing from the passage. Read the article through and decide where the following sentences should go.

1. Now the universities are learning a new trick: if you can't beat 'em, luxuriate 'em.
2. Enjoy it, kids. Once upon a time, all your elders had was a funnel.
3. It's all part of the sales pitch to make collegiate facilities sound as nice as possible.
4. Construction-happy colleges rarely dip into their endowments to pay for their **largesse**.
5. The students are justifiably thrilled with their lavish new surroundings—but they also expect it.

Exercise II   Multiple-Choice Questions

Directions: Complete each of the following statements with the best choice given.

1. Once upon a time, a typical college freshman's day would begin something like _____.
   A. waking up in a creaky dorm room

B. stepping over your roommate's dirty laundry

   C. slumping down the hall to the bathroom

   D. all of the above

2. In today's college, you _____.

   A. brush your teeth next to a total stranger

   B. no longer use words like dorm or cafeteria

   C. step over your roommate in your dorm

   D. get a funny look if you say residence hall, or dining marketplace

3. _____'s new rec facility features an outdoor pool with waterfalls, water slides and a hot tub that seats 20.

   A. The University of North Carolina at Chapel Hill

   B. The University of Houston

   C. Ohio State University

   D. The University of Missouri-Kansas City

4. _____ will pay for those fancy new digs.

   A. The schools

   B. The building users

   C. The government

   D. The community

5. The wine tastings are part of _____'s alcohol-education efforts.

   A. Colby College

   B. the University of Houston

   C. the University of North Carolina

   D. Ohio State University

Exercise III   Word Matching

Directions: Please choose from among the supplied words to explain the original forms of the boldfaced words in the following sentences.

A. horrific   B. persuade   C. unpleasant   D. disadvantage   E. clever

1. Put it this way: colleges no longer use **icky** words like dorm or cafeteria.
2. It was totally weird that a major university had these **horrendous** facilities.
3. At the University of Missouri-Kansas City, the administration just put the finishing touches on its first new residence hall in nearly half a century, the $22 million, 561-bed

Oak Street Hall, a suite-style building wired for the digitally **savvy** freshman.

4. The **downside** is the risk of establishing class divisions on campus.
5. Some schools are even trying to **woo** students with, well, refreshments.

Exercise IV Short-Answer Questions

Directions: Please answer the following questions briefly in your own words.

1. What kind of extracurricular life do today's college students have?
2. "It's no secret that the admissions process has become as ferocious as Tom Cruise in a roomful of psychiatrists." What does this sentence mean?
3. How do you understand the title of this article "which college brings the bling"?

Exercise V Discussion

Directions: Please discuss the following questions in pairs or groups.

1. What do you think of the rec facility on your campus?
2. Do collegiate facilities play an important role in your choice of university?

Text C

Mixed Results on Paying City Students to Pass Tests

By Elissa Gootman

1   Offered up to $1,000 for scoring well on Advanced Placement exams, students at 31 New York City high schools took 345 more of the tests this year than last. But the number who passed declined slightly, raising questions about the effectiveness of increasingly popular pay-for-performance programs in schools here and across the country.

2   Students involved in the program, financed with $2 million in private donations and

aimed at closing a racial gap in Advanced Placement results, posted more 5's, the highest possible score. That rise, however, was overshadowed by a decline in the number of 4's and 3's. Three is the minimum passing score.

3   The effort to reward city students for passing Advanced Placement tests is part of a growing trend nationally and internationally, and one of several new programs in New York, to experiment with using financial incentives to lift attendance and achievement.

4   The results, scheduled to be formally announced on Wednesday, are likely to be closely examined by both enthusiasts who herald such programs as groundbreaking innovation and detractors who deride them as short-sighted bribes that threaten broader educational progress.

5   "I'm just dumbfounded that they can regard this as an achievement or as a great improvement or as something worth spending the money on," said Sol Stern, a senior fellow at the conservative Manhattan Institute, who had expressed cautious support for the Advanced Placement program when it was announced last fall. "I'm surprised that that kind of money, that kind of incentives, doesn't produce better results. It sort of undercuts the argument that the problem is the question of motivation."

6   The organizers and underwriters of the program said they were encouraged by the increase in test-takers and student survey results. They said they never expected to see significant change in the first year, noting that the program was announced after the school year was under way and students had signed up for Advanced Placement classes.

7   "We've gotten off the ground, and we never thought that this was going to be a quick-fix incentive solution," said Edward Rodriguez, executive director of the program, known as Reach, for Rewarding Achievement. "We've learned a great deal about our schools and are figuring out other ways we can support them."

8   While cash-incentive programs are expanding rapidly in schools nationwide—most of them financed by philanthropists—measurable evidence of their effectiveness is scarce. Perhaps the largest such program is starting this fall.

9   In it, corporations and foundations have pledged $79 million over five years to pay 13,000 students and their teachers in 67 high schools in six states $100 for each passing score on the math, science or English Advanced Placement test.

10 The New York effort is modeled on a Texas program that an economist at Cornell found

to be associated with a rise in SAT scores and college enrollments.

11   In Tucson, Ariz., Superintendent Vicki Balentine said that after the first year of a three-year plan to give 75 sophomores $100 per month for maintaining perfect attendance and at least a C minus average, those offered the money seemed to show up more for classes and school activities than a control group.

12   In Coshocton, Ohio, Superintendent David Hire said he saw "significant improvement" over the past four years as the schools gave students who passed state achievement tests "Coshocton bucks," gift certificates that can be redeemed at local stores.

13   "I think it helps the kids take the test more seriously," Dr. Hire said of the program, which has distributed $62,000 of the coupons. "It gives them something to look forward to, and it helps to keep them focused."

14   In New York, in addition to the privately run Advanced Placement program, Roland G. Fryer, a Harvard economist who is serving as the Department of Education's chief equality officer, is leading the school system's effort to give students prizes of up to $50 per test for taking and passing other standardized tests.

15   Officials said on Tuesday that test scores of the nearly 6,000 students who participated in Dr. Fryer's program, which distributed $1.1 million in private donations, would be released in October.

16   Dr. Fryer said that the A.P. test incentive program shed no light on the efficacy of a separate one he is managing that rewards middle school students with cellphone minutes for good behavior, attendance and homework along with test scores.

17   "I crave for scientific evidence that things are working," Dr. Fryer said, adding that while he believed that incentive programs held promise, "the jury is still out."

18   "I don't think we should make too much of the actual numbers at this point, but I'm encouraged that they're trying something," he said of the Advanced Placement program. "I actually don't care if incentives are the answer; I just care about getting an answer. If incentives aren't the answer, I guarantee you I will drop them like a bad habit."

19   Mr. Rodriguez, of Rewarding Achievement, said the Advanced Placement program would be tweaked for next year, and that the rewards for 4's and 3's would most likely be lowered to $500 and $250 (scores of 5 will still net $1,000). He said the money would be better spent to add teacher training sessions and expand a three-day crash course ahead of the exams.

20   Whitney Tilson, who helped create the incentive program and is on the board of the Council of Urban Professionals, which runs it, and the Pershing Square Foundation, its major underwriter, said that he would be "very, very disappointed" if next year's Advanced Placement scores were flat. But he said he hoped more students would sign up as word spread

that the $1,000 promise was for real.

21   The 31 participating schools include six Roman Catholic and 25 public schools, selected based on criteria including minority enrollment and prior student performance on A.P. exams.

22   Performance varied widely. Students at Flushing High School, for example, took 69 more exams this year than last, and passed 44 more, but students at the High School for Arts and Business in Queens passed 10 fewer exams in 2008 than in 2007. Program organizers attributed some lower scores to the departure of veteran teachers in those subjects.

23   In addition to the payments to students, the program offers bonuses to principals and assistant principals and donations to schools where test scores improve. This year, $960,000 was distributed to students.

24   In a written statement, the city Education Department said that officials were still evaluating the results but that "the success of an innovative program like Reach, which insists that every student can succeed, has never been more imperative."

25   At the 31 schools, the number of exams taken rose to 4,620 from 4,275. The number of tests passed fell to 1,476 from 1,481. Kati Haycock, director of the Education Trust, a Washington research group that works on closing the racial achievement gap, said that having five fewer passing A.P. grades was "not exactly a stellar result" but that it was too early to judge the effort.

26   "There's some part of all of us that gets a little queasy at this sort of buying stuff," she said. "That said, the problem of underperformance, especially among poor and minority kids, is so serious and has been with us for so long that I'm not begrudging anybody who has good will here from trying something so we can hopefully learn something from it."

27   "Frankly, rich kids get paid for high grades all the time and for high test scores by their parents," Ms. Haycock added. "So this isn't so different."

(Words: 1272)

Exercise I Discussion

Directions: Please discuss the following questions in pairs or groups.

1. Are these pay-for-performance programs in schools popular in China?
2. What do you think of this phenomenon?
3. Do you believe financial incentives can lift attendance and achievement of students?

Exercise II Writing

Directions: Write a composition in about 150 words, stating your opinion on the pros and cons of the Chinese education system in general or tertiary education in particular with reference to the American education system.

UNIT TWO

ENVIRONMENTAL PROTECTION

Target of the Unit

☞ To get a glimpse of environmental problems the Earth is facing
☞ To practice reading skills
☞ To enlarge your vocabulary

1) LEAD IN

Directions: In this unit, you will read 3 passages about environmental problems and efforts different countries are making to solve them. Read them and try to think of some solutions.

2) DISCUSSION

What does a friendly environment mean to the populace living on the Earth?

Text A

New Orleans Disaster Serves Up a Tough Lesson on Environment

By Richard Ingham

Warming-up Exercises

☞ What environmental problems might a city encounter on its way of development if some vital factors have not been taken into consideration?

First reading

Directions: Now please read the following passage as fast as you can and summarize the main idea.

1 On August 29, Hurricane Katrina swamped New Orleans, a city built below sea level, sustained by a complex system of dams and whose buffer against storm surges, the wetlands of the Mississippi Delta, had been eroded by reckless development.

> **Cajun** *n.* one from Louisiana in the US who has French-Canadian ancestors（祖先从阿卡迪亚迁移来的）法裔路易斯安那州人
> **levee** *n.* an embankment raised to prevent a river from overflowing 护坡，堤
> **boost** *v.* to increase or improve something 提高

2 To most of the world, New Orleans had been the "Big Easy", the cradle of the blues, the home of **Cajun** cooking, and symbol of laid-back style.

3 But to environmental experts, the city had been a disaster just waiting to happen.

4 "We have always used New Orleans as the perfect example of the unsustainable city. It is a hopeless case," Klaus Jacob, senior research scientist at the Lamont-Doherty Earth Observatory at New York's Columbia University, told *AFP*.

5 "The city started to be built in the French Quarter, on high ground, which is the logical place to be when you build a village."

6 "But what happened is that as settlement progressed, people didn't want to be periodically flooded. So a complicated system of **levees** was erected, with pumps and so on, and this allowed the city to develop."

7 "But at the same time, the delta subsided as a result of natural action and the city got lower as the water around it built up."

8 The US Geological Survey (USGS) had warned in vain about preserving the delta wetlands, describing them as a "natural buffer". The progressive loss of this asset heightened the coast's exposure to floods and storms, especially in the light of evidence about global warming, the USGS said.

9  Warming water expands, thus **boosting** sea levels, and also increases the source of energy that feeds hurricanes, making them potentially more vicious.

10   New Orleans may be the most blatant example in the United States of unsustainable development—the term for human activities that eventually carry a huge cost because of environmental damage—but it is certainly not the only one.

> **sloppy** *adj.* not done carefully or thoroughly 草率的
> **shanty** *n.* a small rough hut 小破棚子
> **inundation** *n.* flooding, by the rise and spread of water, of a land surface that is not normally submerged（水）湮没
> **pontoon** *n.* one of several metal containers or boats that are fastened together to support a floating bridge 浮舟，浮码头

11   Other specialists point to coastline cities built on reclaimed wetlands in southern Florida, the most hurricane-prone part of the United States, as well as Los Angeles and cities built in Nevada and Arizona, which need air-conditioning and a long supply line of water to survive.

12   These problems are not, of course, exclusively American.

13   Examples of unsustainable urban development teem on almost every continent—of cities whose poor location, **sloppy** building codes or ill-maintained infrastructure expose them to floods, earthquakes or water stress, or where choking pollution and sprawling **shanty** housing blight the life of its citizens.

14   More than 400 people were killed in Mumbai after the city was lashed by unprecedented monsoon rains in July. Its decrepit drainage system, laid down in the 19th century, could not cope.

15   Yet even sparkling modern cities are flawed. Shanghai, for instance, may be prone to **inundation** because of subsidence, inflicted by the unbridled building of skyscrapers and excess pumping, now curbed, of the water table.

16   Not all the news is bad.

17   Seb Beloe, director of research and advocacy at Sustain Ability, a London consultancy that advises corporations about sustainable development, said worries about climate change were prompting some countries, notably in Europe, to invest more in urban planning and building standards to protect their cities.

18   "A case in point is the Netherlands, which is very low-lying and vulnerable to sea-level rise," he said.

19   "Houses, for instance, are being designed so that they can actually float. They are built on **pontoons**, which rise up from the foundations if the area is flooded."

20   In the United States, the pressure for change is likely to come from business rather than Washington, Beloe predicted.

21   "The US government is in a unique position in that it still questions the science around

global warming and climate change," Beloe said.

22   "But from the US business point of view, it is logical to at least look at the risks."

23   "Insurance premiums in New Orleans, for instance, will be going through the roof. Insurance companies at least recognize that this sort of event is going to be more frequent, even if the federal government doesn't."

(Words: 671)

Second Reading

Directions: Read the text again more carefully to find enough information for Exercises I, II & III.

Exercise I True or False

Directions: Please state whether the following statements are true or false (T/F) according to what you've found in the text.

1. It was wrong to build the city of New Orleans on high ground in the first place.
2. The USGS had warned about preserving the delta wetlands, but it was turned a deaf ear to.
3. Global warming also contributed to the severity of New Orleans' problem.
4. Most coastline cities in the United States are prone to hurricanes.
5. In the case of Mumbai, the old drainage system of the city proved to be a great problem.
6. Shanghai has the same problem with New Orleans in city construction.
7. European countries, notably France, made the first attempts to cope with environmental problems facing their cities.
8. The US government is more reluctant to take actions to invest more in urban planning and building standards to protect their cities.
9. Houses in the Netherlands are built on high ground to avoid flood.
10. We can infer from the article that in the US business rather than the government will first take actions against such events as that of New Orleans.

Exercise II Word Inference

Directions: Often you can guess the meaning of a word/expression by reading the words around it. Please read the given sentence to see how each word/expression in bold type is used in the text. Then choose the answer that is closest in meaning to the bold-faced word/expression.

1. On August 29, Hurricane Katrina swamped New Orleans, a city built below sea level, sustained by a complex system of dams and whose **buffer** against storm surges, the wetlands of the Mississippi Delta, had been eroded by reckless development.
   A. invasion
   B. protection
   C. aggression
   D. position

2. To most of the world, New Orleans had been the "Big Easy", the cradle of the blues, the home of Cajun cooking, and symbol of **laid-back** style.
   A. lazy   B. black
   C. relaxed   D. fun

3. But at the same time, the delta **subsided** as a result of natural action and the city got lower as the water around it built up.
   A. expand
   B. sink
   C. disappear
   D. rise

4. Warming water expands, thus boosting sea levels, and also increases the source of energy that feeds hurricanes, making them potentially more **vicious**.
   A. strong
   B. malicious
   C. harmful
   D. violent

5. New Orleans may be the most **blatant** example in the United States of unsustainable development...
   A. positive   B. obvious
   C. bad   D. good

6. Examples of unsustainable urban development teem on almost every continent—of cities whose poor location,... or where choking pollution and sprawling shanty housing **blight** the life of its citizens.

   A. enrich
   B. damage
   C. impoverish
   D. enliven

7. Its **decrepit** drainage system, laid down in the 19th century, could not cope.

   A. old and decaying
   B. excellent
   C. well-maintained
   D. complicated

8. More than 400 people were killed in Mumbai after the city was **lashed** by unprecedented monsoon rains in July.

   A. visit
   B. wash
   C. clean
   D. hit

9. Yet even sparkling modern cities are flawed. Shanghai, for instance, may be prone to inundation because of subsidence, inflicted by the **unbridled** building of skyscrapers and excess pumping, now curbed, of the water table.

   A. not controlled
   B. enormous
   C. heavy
   D. intense

10. ...said worries about climate change were **prompting** some countries, notably in Europe, to invest more in urban planning and building standards to protect their cities.

    A. help
    B. remind
    C. urge
    D. let

Exercise III Discussion

Directions: Please discuss the following questions in pairs or groups.

1. What are the similarities and differences between New Orleans, Shanghai, and cities in the Netherlands where environmental problems are concerned?
2. What factors should be considered in urban planning and construction?

Text B

Forest Loss in Sumatra Becomes a Global Issue

By Peter Gelling

Warming-up Exercises

☞ Global warming has been one of the most threatening problems that we human beings are facing now. No one wants to see the disaster depicted in *The Day After Tomorrow* happen to us someday in the future. To the best of your knowledge, what are the significant contributing factors to global warming?

• First reading •

Directions: Now please read the following passage as fast as you can and summarize the main idea.

1   KUALA CENAKU, Indonesia, Dec. 1—Here on the island of Sumatra, about 1,200 miles from the global climate talks under way on Bali, are some of the world's fastest-disappearing forests.

2   ___A___.

3   "What can we possibly do to stop this?" said Pak Helman, 28, a villager here in Riau Province, surveying the scene from his leaking wooden longboat. "I feel lost. I feel **abandoned**."

4   In recent years, dozens of pulp and paper companies have descended on Riau, which is roughly the size of Switzerland, snatching up generous government concessions to log and establish palm oil plantations.   **B**   .

> **abandon** *v.* to withdraw one's support or help from, especially in spite of duty, allegiance, or responsibility; desert 放弃，抛弃
> **shrimp** *n.* any of various small, chiefly marine decapod crustaceans of the suborder Natantia, many species of which are edible, having a compressed or elongated body with a well-developed abdomen, long legs and antennae, and a long spinelike projection of the carapace 虾米
> **deforestation** *n.* It refers to the loss of forests due to overcutting of trees. One consequence of deforestation is soil erosion, which results in the loss of protective soil cover and the water-holding capacity of the soil 森林采伐
> **pulp** *v.* to reduce wood, paper and rags to pulp to make paper 制成纸浆

5   Only five years ago, Mr. Helman said, he earned nearly $100 a week catching **shrimp**. Now, he said, logging has poisoned the rivers snaking through the heart of Riau, and he is lucky to find enough shrimp to earn $5 a month.

6
7   **C**   .

Fortunately, from Mr. Helman's point of view, the issue of Riau's disappearing forests has become a global one. He is now a volunteer for Greenpeace, which has established a camp in his village to monitor what it calls an impending Indonesian "carbon bomb."

8   **Deforestation**, during which carbon stored in trees is released into the atmosphere, now accounts for 20 percent of the world's greenhouse gas emissions, according to scientists. And Indonesia releases more carbon dioxide through deforestation than any other country.

9   Within Indonesia, the situation is most critical in Riau. In the past 10 years, nearly 60 percent of the province's forests have been logged, burned and **pulped**, according to Jikalahari, a local environmental group.

10   "This is very serious—the world needs to act now," said Susanto Kurniawan, a coordinator

for Jikalahari who regularly makes the arduous trip into the forest from the nearby city of Pekanbaru, passing long lines of trucks carting palm oil and wood. "In a few years it will be too late."

> **swath** *n.* the space created by the swing of a scythe or the cut of a mowing machine 镰刀或割草机割过后留下的地方，此处借指砍伐树木后留下的一片片空地
> **peatland** *n.* The simple definition of a peatland is an area where peat is found. Peat, or turf as it is often called in Ireland, is a type of soil that contains a high proportion of dead organic matter, mainly plants, that has accumulated over thousands of years. Close inspection can reveal the types of plants that grew, died and accumulated to form a piece of peat. 泥炭地
> **degradation** *n.* a decline to a lower condition, quality, or level 退化
> **skeptic** *n.* a person who habitually doubts generally accepted beliefs 怀疑者
> **acquit** *v.* to free or clear from a charge or accusation 无罪释放

11   __D__ . But its use is causing more harm than good, environmental groups say, because companies slash and burn huge **swaths** of trees to make way for palm oil plantations.

12   Even more significant, the burning and drying of Riau's carbon-rich **peatlands**, also to make way for palm oil plantations, releases about 1.8 billion tons of greenhouse gases a year, according to Greenpeace officials.

13   But it is also in Riau that a new global strategy for conserving forests in developing countries might begin. A small area of Riau's remaining forest will become a test case if an international carbon-trading plan called REDD is adopted.

14   REDD, or Reducing Emissions from Deforestation and Forest **Degradation**, is to be one of the central topics of discussion at the Bali conference. __E__ .

15   Indonesia, caught between its own financial interest in the palm oil industry and the growing international demands for conservation, has been promoting the carbon-trading plan for months.

16   But there are plenty of **skeptics**, who doubt it will be possible to measure just how much carbon is being conserved—and who question whether the lands involved can be protected from illegal logging and corruption.

17   Illegal logging is commonplace in Indonesia, and though the government has prosecuted dozens of cases in recent years, it says it cannot be everywhere. Companies in this remote area are cultivating land legally sold to them by the Indonesian government, but maps of their projects obtained by Greenpeace indicate that many of them have also moved into protected areas.

18   Critics say corruption is their biggest concern. The most famous illegal logger in Indonesia, Adelin Lis, who operated in North Sumatra, was arrested this year, only to be **acquitted** by a court in Medan, the provincial capital. He then left the country.

19   The attorney general's office has opened a corruption investigation into judges and the police in Medan, and says there are many similar cases. "There are a number of ongoing investigations into corruption that has allowed illegal **loggers** from all over Indonesia to go free," said Thomson Siagian, a spokesman for the attorney general. "In such a lucrative industry, payoffs are common."

> **logger** *n.* one who logs trees; a lumberjack 伐木工
> **ferry** *v.* to transport (people, vehicles, or goods) by boat across a body of water 摆渡
> **tinker** *v.* to make small changes to something in order to repair it or make it work better 鼓捣

20   At the Bali conference, the Woods Hole Research Center, an environmental group based in the United States, has presented research showing that new satellite technology can make it more feasible to track illegal logging. Reports "show that radar imagery from new sensors recently placed in orbit can solve the problem of monitoring reductions in tropical deforestation, which previously was a major obstacle because of cloud cover that optical sensors can't see through," said John P. Holdren, the center's director.

21   Such developments are good news to Mr. Helman, the villager in Riau who, using his wooden boat, has been **ferrying** a steady stream of foreign environmentalists and journalists in and out of the forest in recent weeks.

22   "I am so thankful for the recent attention," he said, **tinkering** with the sputtering engine. "At times it seems too late. But I see some hope now."

(Words: 904)

Second Reading

Directions: Read the text again more carefully to find enough information for Exercises I, II, III, IV & V.

Exercise I Understanding Text Organization

Directions: You may find there are a few sentences (segments) missing from the passage. Read the article through and decide where the following sentences should go.

1. Responding to global demand for palm oil, which is used in cooking and cosmetics and, lately, in an increasingly popular biodiesel, companies have been claiming any land they can.

2. The results have caused villagers to feel panic.

3. Essentially, it would involve payments by wealthy countries to developing countries for every hectare of forest they do not cut down.
4. A look at this vast wasteland of charred stumps and dried-out peat makes the fight to save Indonesia's forests seem nearly impossible.
5. The rate of this deforestation is rising as oil prices reach new highs, leading more industries to turn to biodiesel made from palm oil, which, in theory, is earth-friendly.

Exercise II Multiple-Choice Questions

Directions: Please choose the best answer to the following questions.

1. Why do the villagers feel panic?
   A. Because they are harvesting less fish than before.
   B. Because they are losing their property.
   C. Because over-logging and the establishment of palm oil plantations are killing their forests and they're losing their livelihood.
   D. Because the establishment of palm oil plantations deprived them of their job opportunities.
2. How many percent of Riau's forests have been logged, burned and pulped in the past 10 years?
   A. 60.
   B. 20.
   C. 40.
   D. 80.
3. What are the industries doing as oil prices reach new highs?
   A. They are importing from overseas market.
   B. Many of them are turning to biodiesel made from palm oil.
   C. Many of them are overlogging.
   D. Many of them are turning to Greenpeace for help.
4. What is the contribution of new satellite technology?
   A. It helps to cover the cloud that ensures enough rainfall.
   B. It makes it easier to track illegal logging.
   C. It helps to put new sensors into orbit.
   D. It helps to monitor reductions in tropical reforestation.

5. What is the attitude of Mr. Helman?

   A. He is worried about the deforestation in his hometown.

   B. He feels panic sometimes but optimistic now.

   C. He believes he should do something to protect the forests in his hometown.

   D. All of the above.

Exercise III   Word Matching

Directions: Please choose from among the supplied words to explain the original forms of the boldfaced words in the following sentences.

A. rights   B. bribes   C. flowing   D. spluttering   E. upcoming

1. Now, he said, logging has poisoned the rivers **snaking** through the heart of Riau, and...

2. In recent years, dozens of pulp and paper companies have descended on Riau, which is roughly the size of Switzerland, snatching up generous government **concessions** to log and establish palm oil plantations.

3. He is now a volunteer for Greenpeace, which has established a camp in his village to monitor what it calls an **impending** Indonesian "carbon bomb."

4. In such a lucrative industry, **payoffs** are common.

5. I am so thankful for the recent attention," he said, tinkering with the **sputtering** engine.

Exercise IV   Short-Answer Questions

Directions: Please answer the following questions briefly in your own words.

1. What does "carbon bomb" mean?

2. A small area of Riau's remaining forest will become a test case if an international carbon-trading plan called REDD is adopted. Do you have any idea about how this will work?

3. Why do critics say corruption is their biggest concern?

Exercise V   Discussion

Directions: Please discuss the following questions in pairs or groups.

1. Do you believe what is under discussion at the Bali conference will be an effective

way to slow overlogging and forest degradation? If not, what is your suggestion?

2. Will you work as a volunteer to advocate for the conservation of tropical forests?

Text C

Nine States in Plan to Cut Emissions by Power Plant

By Anthony DePalma

1   Officials in New York and eight other Northeastern states have come to a preliminary agreement to freeze power plant emissions at their current levels and then reduce them by 10 percent by 2020, according to a confidential draft proposal.

2   The cooperative action, the first of its kind in the nation, came after the Bush administration decided not to regulate the greenhouse gases that contribute to global warming. Once a final agreement is reached, the legislatures of the nine states will have to enact it, which is considered likely.

3   Enforcement of emission controls could potentially result in higher energy prices in the nine states, which officials hope can be offset by subsidies and support for the development of new technology that would be paid for with the proceeds from the sale of emission allowances to the utility companies.

4   The regional initiative would set up a market-driven system to control emissions of carbon dioxide, the main greenhouse gas, from more than 600 electric generators in the nine states. Environmentalists who support a federal law to control greenhouse gases believe that the model established by the Northeastern states will be followed by other states, resulting in pressure that could eventually lead to the enactment of a national law.

5   California, Washington and Oregon are in the early stages of exploring a regional agreement similar to the Northeastern plan. The nine states in the Northeastern agreement are Connecticut, Delaware, Maine, Massachusetts, New Hampshire, New Jersey, New York, Rhode Island and Vermont. They were brought together in 2003 by a Republican governor, George E. Pataki of New York, who broke sharply and openly with the Bush administration over the handling of greenhouse gases and Washington's refusal to join more than 150 countries in signing the Kyoto Protocols, the agreement to reduce emissions that went into

effect earlier this year.

6   Mr. Pataki, who may be considering a run for the Republican nomination for president, has refrained from criticizing President Bush directly, but he has repeatedly said that the states need to act on their own even if the Bush administration has not made the issue a priority.

7   Preliminary details of the region's emission reduction goals were included in a confidential memo circulated among officials of all nine states that was given to *The New York Times* by a person who supports the enactment of national legislation to control emissions, but who did not want to be identified because he was not authorized to have the memo.

8   Andrew Rush, a spokesman for Governor Pataki, declined to comment on the draft because it was not a final document. However, he said, "a tremendous amount of progress has been made and we look forward to continuing to work with the other states so that we can reach a final agreement that will build on the governor's strong record of protecting the environment and reducing harmful emissions."

9   Samuel Wolfe, assistant commissioner for the New Jersey Department of Environmental Protection, who has been actively involved in the negotiations, said that there is still work to be done on the proposal but that "the states are working very productively to resolve the issues and we have very high hopes of getting a resolution through to all the states by the end of September."

10 In a statement, James L. Connaughton, chairman of the White House Council on Environmental Quality, tried to put the states' initiative in a positive light. "We welcome all efforts to help meet the president's goal for significantly reducing greenhouse gas intensity by investing in new, more efficient technologies," he said.

11   In recent years, New York and other Northeastern states have aggressively tried to reduce power plant emissions. Several have joined together to sue coal-fired power plants in Midwestern states that produce sulfur dioxide and nitrogen oxide that drift across state borders and cause acid rain in the Northeast.

12   The Northeastern region is itself a substantial producer of greenhouse gases. Environmental groups calculate that the region's carbon dioxide emissions are roughly equivalent to those of Germany.

13   While any reductions achieved in the region would be significant, environmentalists believe that the real importance of the cooperative effort is in the example it sets for other states.

14   "We're not going to solve the problem of global warming in the Northeastern states," said Dale S. Bryk, a senior attorney with the Natural Resources Defense Council who has been watching the regional effort since it was proposed by Governor Pataki in a letter to the other governors in April 2003. "But we're showing that we have the American ingenuity to do this and we're setting a precedent in terms of the design of the program."

15   As outlined in the draft, the regional carbon dioxide control plan would set specific caps on emissions that would drop over time.

16   The hope is that by providing long-range incentives for the electric generating companies to comply, the program will make improvements more cost-effective.

17   Emissions would be capped at 150 million tons of carbon dioxide a year, a figure that is about equal to the average emissions in the highest three years between 2000 and 2004. Each of the nine states would have its own cap. New York's, at 65.6 million tons, would be the largest. Vermont's would be the smallest, with 1.35 million tons.

18   The caps would be enforced starting in 2009. By that time, restricting emissions to levels prevailing now would, in effect, require a reduction of emissions relative to power output, because electric generation is expected to increase between now and then. The 150 million-ton cap would be sustained through 2015, when reductions would be required, reaching 10 percent in 2020. The Kyoto protocol freezes emissions at the 1990 level and imposes a 7 percent reduction in 2012.

19   Environmentalists say there are too many variables involved to directly compare the two programs, but they are believed to achieve roughly the same kind of carbon reductions. However, some environmentalists are disappointed with the draft plan. They argue that much deeper cuts were achievable.

20   "It's good that they are going to be talking about actual reductions," said Robert J. Moore, executive director of Environmental Advocates of New York. "However,

the targets that are being contemplated, though a positive step, are somewhat less than ambitious."

21   Gavin J. Donohue, president of the Independent Power Producers of New York, said that meeting the proposed caps "would be very difficult" for electric generators in New York, especially now that the price of oil has soared.

22   Mr. Donohue, who once worked for Governor Pataki in the Department of Environmental Conservation, said that his principal concern was assuring that the limits will not put electric generators in New York and the other states at a competitive disadvantage with states that were not constrained.

23   The Bush administration's rejection of the Kyoto Protocols has caused deep divisions nationwide, with many local governments attempting to force the administration to taking action by passing their own carbon dioxide rules.

24   Earlier this year, for example, the mayors of more than 130 cities, including New York and Los Angeles, joined in a bipartisan coalition to fight global warming on a local level by agreeing to meet the emissions reductions contained in the international pact.

25   One part of the proposal that is not yet final deals with the sale of emission allowances under a cap-and-trade system. Such systems allow generating companies that have not used all of their emission quotas to sell the right to emit more pollution to competitors. In this way, the total amount of pollution can be controlled, while the economic viability of the companies is protected.

26   When this system was used in Europe, the carbon dioxide allowances were given to the generating companies. The Northeastern states are considering withholding some allowances and selling them to the generating companies.

(Words: 1307)

Exercise I Discussion

Directions: Please discuss the following questions in pairs or groups.

1. What might be the consequences of the enactment of the emission control according to the article?
2. What are the reasons for the nine states to take cooperative action against power plant?
3. What are the steps the nine states will take?

Exercise II Writing

Directions: Write a composition in about 150 words, telling what developed countries should do to protect the environment or what China has already done based on the research you've done.

UNIT THREE

CHINA HORIZONS

Target of the Unit

☞ To get a glimpse of modern Chinese society from a foreigner's perspective
☞ To practice reading skills
☞ To enlarge your vocabulary

1) LEAD IN

Directions: In this unit, you will read 3 passages about what is happening in China. All of them are from foreign media. Read them critically and see whether you agree with the ideas expressed in them.

2) DISCUSSION

To your knowledge, what was China like before in the eye of the Americans or other foreigners? How about now?

Text A

Numbers Game in China

By Jim Yardley

Warming-up Exercises

☞ What do you think of the idea that a nice car should get a nice license plate?
☞ Can you give some examples of superstitions on numerology?

• First reading •

Directions: Now please read the following passage as fast as you can and summarize the main idea.

1   GUANGZHOU, China—At a government **auction** inside a badminton gymnasium, a young businessman named Ding walked away a happy winner. Like everyone else, he was bidding on license plates and did not seem to mind that has cost 54,000 *yuan*.

> **auction** *n.* a public sale in which property or items of merchandise are sold to the highest bidder 拍卖
> **bonkers** *adj.* crazy 疯狂的
> **potent** *adj.* exerting or capable of exerting strong influence 有影响力的
> **superstition** *n.* a belief, practice, or rite irrationally maintained by ignorance of the laws of nature or by faith in magic or chance 迷信

2   For nearly the same money, which is the equivalent of $6,750, Ding could have afforded two of the Chinese-made roadsters popular in the domestic car market. His bid was almost 13 times what a Chinese farmer earns in a year, and almost 2.9 times the country's per capita annual income.

3   And yet, in the recent auction in this manufacturing capital in southern China, Ding could not even claim top price. The most expensive plate, AC6688, fetched 80,000 *yuan* on a day when officials sold 200 plates for 2,932,000 *yuan*, or $366,500.

4   "I thought it was rather cheap," said Ding, 30, a gold chain glinting under his open black sport shirt, as he walked off with the paperwork for APY888. "Since I have a nice car, I thought I should get a nice plate."

5   No country is more **bonkers** over cars than China, where achieving the new middle-class dream means owning a shiny new vehicle. But the car is not always enough for those who aspire beyond the middle class. A license plate has become almost as much of a status symbol as the car itself.

6   The reason is the **potent** blend of new-money aspirations and Old World **superstitions**. For centuries, numbers have served as a second language in China. The unluckiest number, 4, or *si*, which can also mean death in Chinese, is so dreaded that some buildings do not have a fourth floor. The luckiest number is 8, or *ba*, which rhymes with *fa*, the Chinese character for

wealth.

7 License plates are usually issued randomly. But in a country where 100,000 people die annually in traffic accidents, a plate that ends in 4 is considered a very bad **omen** for a superstitious motorist; it might as well read DEATH. A plate **overflowing** with 8s would portend good fortune.

> **omen** *n.* a phenomenon supposed to portend good or evil; a prophetic sign 预兆
> **overflow** *v.* to have a boundless supply; be superabundant 充满, 洋溢
> **infatuation** *n.* a foolish, unreasoning, or extravagant passion or attraction 沉迷

8 Not willing to leave owning a lucky plate merely to luck itself, many people have tried to buy them, whether as a sort of supernatural insurance policy or simply to flaunt their wealth. Bribery has arisen in several cities as officials have traded favorable plates for stuffed envelopes. Entrepreneurs also have tried to cash in: A man in the city of Hangzhou placed an Internet ad offering to sell his plate of A88888 for 1.12 million *yuan*.

9 The aroma of corruption was enough that officials in Guangzhou decided to put the plates up for public auction and announced that proceeds would be dedicated to help accident victims. A few other cities have also started auctions.

10 Zhao Shu, chairman of the China Folk Art and Literature Association, said the **infatuation** with lucky plates was a gross distortion of traditional Chinese culture. "People are feeling empty and superficial," Zhao said. "They are not learning the traditional culture and they misunderstand it."

11 "It shows a very superficial culture. It's bragging by the new rich."

12 Zhao, who said the symbolism of numbers traces to Confucius as well as Taoism, said the current emphasis on 8 and 4 was misguided and overlooked the fact that no number was considered solely lucky or unlucky. He said that a proper interpretation of numbers was far more nuanced and linked in meaning to the spoken language itself. And good fortune, he added, cannot be purchased with a bundle of 8s.

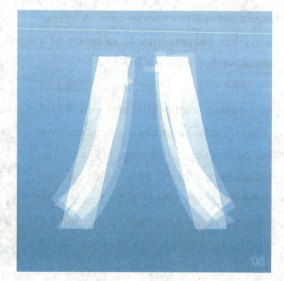

13 "What we are seeing today is a return to the traditional culture, " he said. "But they got it wrong."

14 Yet, if anything, the public infatuation with numbers is growing. Cellphone stores offer "lucky" numbers, some of which

cost as much as 16,000 *yuan*. A regional Chinese airline reportedly paid about 2.4 million *yuan*, or $300,000, to have 8888 8888 for a telephone number. Chinese newspapers reported that some parents refused to let their children ride taxis with "unlucky" license plates en route to taking the national college entrance exam.

> **numerology** *n.* the study of the occult meanings of numbers and their supposed influence on human life. 数字命理学
> **paddle** *n.* a small wooden instrument used at an auction 竞拍牌

15   China tried to stamp out superstition but never succeeded and now **numerology** is just one of the superstitions that can make for a profitable consulting business. Some Chinese companies seek out such advice on product names, or about which floor of a building to open an office, or to determine whether the boss has a lucky or unlucky telephone number.

16   "People have more money now and they want to spend it to get more luck," said Fang Mingyuan, who works in a Guangzhou agency that has provided such advice.

17   The auction in Guangzhou, the city's third, was held on Ersha Island, which has become home to some of the city's wealthiest people. About 200 people arrived on a broiling day, registered their banking information and were assigned a numbered auction **paddle**. Outside, the parking lot was stuffed with BMWs, Volvos, Audis and Jaguars, a few of which had arrived from the showroom floor without a license plate.

18   "Welcome on such a hot day," said the auctioneer, a government official in a shiny black suit. "I wish you a successful afternoon." For good measure, he added: "And I wish you luck on gambling on the World Cup."

19   There was no shouting, no barking from the auctioneer. A few titters arose whenever a bidding war broke out. Some bidders were merely drivers representing their bosses. "He didn't want a specific plate number, but he said that 20,000 *yuan* was the maximum," said Liao Ruibin of his boss's willingness to spend the equivalent of $2,500. "He has a Mercedes."

20   Liao ended up spending about 11,000 *yuan* of his boss's money for APL238. "He has an expensive car and wants an expensive plate to match."

21   A woman who spent 23,000 *yuan* on APX333 said of the custom plates, "All my friends have them." Meanwhile, Ding, the salesman who spent $6,750, said that his friends "all have BMWs and Mercedes" and that "they all have good plates." His car is a new Chrysler and he said he considered his new plate a necessity.

22   Not everyone wanted the most expensive plates. Lu Yao, 21, said anytime "you see a nice car with four of five 8s, people know they must be rich." She and her parents paid about 11,000 *yuan* for APL128, a number that matched her birthday. Hours earlier, her mother had surprised her father with a sport utility vehicle, and the family had arrived directly from the

sales lot.

23   "It's all these superstitions," said Lu, who attends college in California. "Apparently, my parents believe in it. We're Confucian. We believe in luck and numbers."

24   Lu said the new car, as well as the plate, were about more than showing off for her family, which has prospered by owning several restaurants. We only got our first car five years ago," she said." My dad couldn't even imagine having a car. He thinks now that he is dreaming.

25   "He started smiling at 10 this morning," she said, "and he still hasn't stopped."

(Words: 1189)

Second Reading

Directions: Read the text again more carefully to find enough information for Exercises I, II & III.

Exercise I True or False

Directions: Please state whether the following statements are true or not (T/F) according to the text.

1. Ding bid on license plates and didn't mind it cost him a lot.
2. His bid could have afforded two of the Chinese-made roadsters and was almost 200 times what a Chinese farmer earns in a year.
3. Ding's bid was the top price in the recent auction in Guangzhou.
4. Owning a car is not always enough for those who aspire beyond the middle class.
5. License plates are usually issued with different fixed prices.
6. A license plate has become almost as much of a status symbol as the car itself because of old superstition.
7. The current emphasis on 8 and 4 was misguided and overlooked the fact that no number was considered solely lucky or unlucky.
8. Numerology is just one of the superstitions that can make for a profitable consulting business now.
9. Everyone wanted the most expensive plates.
10. It is a common phenomenon that a nice car goes with a nice plate.

Exercise II Word Inference

Directions: Often you can guess the meaning of a word/expression by reading the words around it. Please read the given sentence to see how each word/expression in bold type is used in the text. Then choose the answer that is closest in meaning to the bold-faced word/expression.

1. He was **bidding** on license plates and did not seem to mind that his cost 54,000 *yuan*.
   A. order
   B. command
   C. behest
   D. offer to pay

2. At a government auction inside a **dingy** badminton gymnasium, a young businessman named Ding walked away a happy winner.
   A. dent   B. hot
   C. dark and dirty   D. humid

3. Ding could have afforded two of the Chinese-made **roadsters** popular in the domestic car market.
   A. roaster
   B. automobile
   C. sports car
   D. roller skate

4. The **aroma** of corruption was enough that officials in Guangzhou decided to put the plates up for public auction.
   A. odor   B. smell
   C. aura   D. phenomenon

5. The infatuation with lucky plates was a gross **distortion** of traditional Chinese culture.
   A. misunderstanding
   B. misleading
   C. misrepresentation
   D. disregard

6. Some parents refused to let their children ride taxis with "unlucky" license plates **en route** to taking the national college entrance exam.
   A. on the way   B. route to
   C. in the way   D. off the way

7. Lu said the new car, as well as the plate, were about more than showing off for her family, which has **prospered** by owning several restaurants.
   A. been luxuriant   B. grown rich
   C. developed   D. made progress

8. A proper interpretation of numbers was far more **nuanced**.
   A. subtle   B. annoyed
   C. slight   D. mistaken

9. Many people have tried to buy them, whether as a sort of supernatural insurance policy or simply to **flaunt** their wealth.
   A. make fun of   B. fluke
   C. show off   D. flounder

10. A plate overflowing with 8s would **portend** good fortune.
    A. pretend   B. predict
    C. have   D. present

Exercise III   Discussion
Directions: Please discuss the following questions in pairs or groups.

1. What do you think of numerology?
2. Does this "numbers game" exist in other cultures? Please gather more information and share with your classmates.

Text B

New Wealth Buys Makeovers in China
By Alexa Olesen

Warming-up Exercises

☞ What do you know about cosmetic surgery?
☞ Do you mind if your boyfriend or girlfriend buys this makeover?

• First reading •

Directions: Now please read the following passage as fast as you can and summarize the main idea.

1   CHANGSHA, China—__A__. Forty pounds lighter, jaw slimmer, eyes and nose refined, breasts lifted, 30-year-old Chen Jing has just been through an extreme **makeover** for a Chinese reality show called "Lovely Cinderella."

2   It's a sharp insight into China's own makeover, as a consumer generation moves ever further from past era of drab-is-beautiful **austerity**.

3   Modeled after "The Swan," Fox TV's reality television show, "Lovely Cinderella" was created in south China's Hunan province and has tapped into a surging Chinese interest in **cosmetics** and cosmetic surgery—luxuries beyond the means of most a generation ago, but gaining in popularity as incomes grow.

makeover *n.* an overall treatment to improve the appearance or change the image 变脸，整容
austerity *n.* an austere habit or practice 苦行，节制的习惯或实践
cosmetics *n.* a preparation, such as powder or a skin cream, designed to beautify the body by direct application 化妆品
Caucasian *n.* anything from the Caucasus region; peoples of the Caucasus, humans from the Caucasus region; languages of the Caucasus; languages spoken in the Caucasus region 高加索人，白人；高加索语言
primp *v.* (old-fashioned) to make yourself look attractive by arranging your hair, putting on make-up etc. 梳洗打扮

4   __B__. They no longer chasing Hollywood's notion of perfection but opting for their own traditional aesthetic.

5   Zhang Xiaomei, a publisher of fashion magazines in Beijing, says, "It was popular to do a surgery 10 years ago, a so-called European-style double eyelid that really made eyes sort of pop and appear more **Caucasian** but it didn't look good and Chinese women have learned from that."

6   High noses and super-plump pouts have also fallen out of favor, she said, giving way to techniques that play up, instead of distort Asian beauty.

7   Asked whom they wanted to look like, "Cinderella" contestants rattled off only Asian names: Li Jiaxin, a former Miss Hong Kong; actress Maggie Cheung; and Kim Hee-sun, a South Korean soap opera star.

8   This full embrace of beauty is a contrast to 30 years ago when even **primping** could be seen as counterrevolutionary. Watching the taping of "Cinderella" with approval, Lu Zaining, mother of beautician Chen, agreed things had changed.

9 "People then would have criticized you for putting on lipstick," she said. "Back then, we couldn't imagine having a television."

10 ___C___. And in plastic surgeon Li Fannian's Yahan Cosmetic Surgery Clinic, posters for implants called Magic Peach and Dream Xcell show ivory-skinned women with bursting **cleavage**.

> **cleavage** *n.* the space between a woman's breasts, as revealed by a low-cut dress 乳沟

11 The clinic's most commonly performed surgeries are minimizing eye bags, sculpting noses and shaving the jawbone to soften the face.

12 Chinese ideas of physical perfection today jibe with ideals espoused for centuries in Chinese literature and art, Li said, describing wide, bright eyes and a face "shaped like a goose egg or a sunflower seed."

13 Double eyelid techniques today are much more subtle and give the appearance of larger eyes, he said, but do not try to make Asian women look Caucasian.

14 "Cinderella" contestant Yang Shaqin, a Beijing undergraduate, said she always wanted to look more like her mother. After eight procedures, she no longer felt like an ugly duckling but insisted she would never date a man shallow enough to have cosmetic surgery.

15 "We have a Chinese saying, 'A man should possess talents and a woman grace,'" Yang said. "Men shouldn't be worried about these trivial sorts of things."

16 ___D___. And Chinese men are also not shy about using products and sometimes surgery to look better.

17 About 10 percent of the clients at the Yahan clinic are men. They spend an average of $10 a month on grooming products, according to a report in the official Xinhua News Agency in December.

18 Zhang, the publisher, estimates there are about 1 million plastic surgeries a year in China. In the United States, with less than a quarter of China's population of 1.3 billion, twice as many operations were performed in 2005.

19 Hao Lulu, a Beijing fashion writer and aspiring actress, became a sensation in the Chinese media—which dubbed her the "Artificial Beauty"—after she had 16 surgeries to redo her eyes, lips, nose, cheeks, neck, breasts, upper arms, buttocks, thighs and calves.

20 ___E___. Last year, a military-run

hospital announced it had become the second facility in the world after France to attempt a complex partial face transplant—grafting a donated nose, upper lip, cheek and eyebrow onto a farmer who had been mauled by a black bear.

> **harrowing** *adj.* extremely distressing; agonizing 令人极其痛苦的，极其苦恼的
> **spoke** *n.* one of the rods or braces connecting the hub and rim of a wheel（自行车）辐条
> **jab** *v.* to stab or pierce 刺入或刺穿
> **footage** *n.* film that has been shot 片子（原义是电影胶片）
> **anesthetic** *n.* a substance that causes lack of feeling or awareness; a general anesthetic puts the person to sleep 麻醉剂

21   The risks some take for beauty can be **harrowing**, especially in an industry that lacks regulation.

22   Wang Junhong, a 37-year-old fashion retailer from Guangzhou in south China's Guangdong province, collected elegant European trousers that she adored but couldn't wear because she was only 5 feet 2 inches tall.

23   So she spent $9,700 to gain two inches in a procedure that involved breaking her legs, driving pins into the bone and gradually cranking the pins apart to lengthen the bones as they heal.

24   "The more I thought about doing it, the more I was convinced I had to do it," said Wang, as she lay in a hospital bed in 2005, her legs encased in brutal-looking frames with **spokes** that **jabbed** through her legs.

25   Height increases job prospects and help-wanted ads sometimes stipulate the requirements for white-collar posts.

26   "Taller people will have more opportunity for promotion," said Sun Honggang, an editor for Human Capital and Career Post, a Beijing newspaper dedicated to employee recruitment.

27   "Lovely Cinderella" producer Wang Zhiyi said that while his show is meant as entertainment, it's also cautionary. The **footage** is graphic, showing grotesquely swollen postoperative faces and surgeons vigorously sucking fat from a contestant's waist.

28   A video clip shows Chen, the beautician, crying out on the operating table for her husband and for more **anesthetic**. Later, she is shown throwing up and weeping in her hospital room because she misses her 5-year-old son.

29   But as she gazes at herself in front of the studio audience, the memories seem to evaporate like the theatrical fog blasted out of fire extinguishers before she stepped to the mirror.

30   "I think that people today, with their more liberal ways of thinking, are at a place where if someone has an opportunity to change their life and become more confident, then everyone would want to support that."

31   Xinhua cited a survey of 2,239 men aged 18 to 60 in seven Chinese cities that found men in Shanghai to be the country's most vain because they spent just over 17 minutes a day gazing in the mirror.

32   Men and women together spent $12 billion on beauty products in 2005, up 13 percent from the previous year, according to the China Association of Perfume, Essence and Cosmetics Industry.

33   The United States Cosmetic, Fragrance, and Toiletry Association last year called China its "largest future growth market," and companies like Avon Products Inc., Mary Kay Inc., L'Oreal SA, and Procter & Gamble Co. are all fighting for a share.

(Words: 1160)

· Second Reading ·

Directions: Read the text again more carefully to find enough information for Exercises I, II, III, IV & V.

Exercise I Understanding Text Organization

Directions: You may find there are a few sentences (segments) missing from the passage. Read the article through and decide where the following sentences should go.

1. These trivial things are driving a booming industry
2. China, which had virtually no cosmetic surgery a few decades ago, now claims to be an innovator
3. Consumers have quickly developed their own tastes
4. The beautician from Chairman Mao's hometown looks at herself in the mirror and bursts into tears of joy
5. In the southern city of Changsha, where "Cinderella" is taped, spas offer seaweed wraps and slimming massages

Exercise II Multiple-Choice Questions

Directions: Please choose the best answer from the four choices given.

1. It's a sharp insight into China's own makeover, as a consumer generation moves ever further from past era of _____. Which of the four choices is **NOT** correct?
   A. disregard of beauty
   B. showing a severe attitude towards makeover
   C. plain is beautiful
   D. ugliness

2. High noses and super-plump pouts have also fallen out of favor, she said, giving way to techniques that _____, instead of distort Asian beauty. Which explanation of the underlined word is suitable?
   A. emphasize
   B. make fun of
   C. play on
   D. set up

3. According to the author, Chinese ideas of physical perfection today _____ ideals espoused for centuries in Chinese literature and art.
   A. agree with
   B. disagree with
   C. laugh at
   D. make fun of

4. The risks some take for beauty can be harrowing, especially in an industry that _____.
   A. develops well
   B. is well regulated
   C. lacks regulation
   D. develops blindly

5. Chen, the beautician, crying out on the operating table for her husband and for more anesthetic and became _____ when she looked at the mirror.
   A. disappointed
   B. angry
   C. sad
   D. exhilarated

Exercise III Word Matching

Directions: Please choose from among the supplied words to explain the original forms of the boldfaced words in the following sentences.

A. approved   B. preening   C. highlight   D. observation   E. are in accord with

1. It's a sharp **insight** into China's own makeover, as a consumer generation moves ever further from past era of drab-is-beautiful austerity.
2. High noses and super-plump pouts have also fallen out of favor, she said, giving way to techniques that **play up**, instead of distort Asian beauty.
3. Chinese ideas of physical perfection today **jibe with** ideals espoused for centuries in Chinese literature and art, Li said, describing wide, bright eyes and a face "shaped like a goose egg or a sunflower seed."
4. Chinese ideas of physical perfection today jibe with ideals **espoused** for centuries in Chinese literature and art, Li said, describing wide, bright eyes and a face "shaped like a goose egg or a sunflower seed."
5. They spend an average of $10 a month on **grooming** products, according to a report in the official Xinhua News Agency in December.

Exercise IV Short-Answer Questions

Directions: Please answer the following questions briefly in your own words.

1. What are the most commonly performed surgeries at the clinic?
2. How important height is in job-hunting? Can you give some examples?
3. Why the United States Cosmetic, Fragrance, and Toiletry Association last year called China its "largest future growth market"?

Exercise V Discussion

Directions: Please discuss the following questions in pairs or groups.

1. The author mentioned in the article that it's a sharp insight into China's own makeover, as a consumer generation moves ever further from past era of drab-is-beautiful austerity. How do you understand it? Ask your parents what their feelings about this change are.
2. Do you believe cosmetic surgery can change a person's fate? Why?

Text C

New Struggle in China: Keep Up with the Chans

By Robert Marquand

1 BEIJING—As the "year of the dog" arrives in China, a new fad for those partaking in China's success is weekend skiing. City-dwellers migrate to one of eight new ski "villages" outside Beijing. Many arrive in SUVs, the current "it" car also used for fashionable expeditions to outbacks in Gansu or inner Mongolia.

2 Chinese who can afford such luxuries are expectation-setters. Along with Olympic games and space launches, they are models of what China can deliver—a prosperous society that President Hu said in his New Year's message will allow "all Chinese to benefit."

3 Yet officials worry that expectations may have risen too fast. Frustration is felt broadly among those who rub shoulders with wealth but aren't quite benefiting. At Beitang Catholic Cathedral on Christmas Eve, Bishop Liu Yongbin appealed to a packed house that "we do not become angry when we see others have more than we do."

4 After 15 years of headlong marketization and material progress, China is at a transitional moment. Its leaders face the delicate task of managing a social contract that includes rising expectations—as well as adapting the political system and Confucian culture to the needs of an increasingly modern and educated populace, experts say.

5 "Things have gone from all ideology and no materialism to all materialism and no ideology or values," notes veteran China watcher Laurence Brahm, owner of the Red Capital Club in Beijing. "Expectations are a big phenomenon. The '80s were about idealism. Now the talk is 'what brand are you using?' Urban China is about keeping up with the Joneses, or the Chans, in this case."

6 To be sure, the hopes of ordinary Chinese have never percolated more strongly. Li Wan, just off the train from Jiangxi province, sits at a huge public electronic "jobs board" downtown that flashes ads for "parking lot attendant" or "deputy office manager." He wears the tan socks and slightly bewildered expression of the waidi, or "outside Beijing person." His dream is an apartment in Beijing and school for his daughter. But like so many interviewed for this story, Mr. Li's plans hinge on making $150 more per month, and work is harder to find than he thought.

7 Around the corner, a young woman chews a chicken sandwich and tells of moving from a Wal-Mart job in Shenzhen to employment as a cosmetics salesperson at Dangdang, an online

shop. She hasn't reached her dream of buying a house and getting married. By law, 10 percent of her earnings go into a housing fund she can tap when she is ready. "I hope my job will be better, and I can buy a house in two years. Many people are waiting to afford a house."

8   In just two decades, China has moved from almost zero productivity and capital, and a state-planned society, to being a top manufacturer with massive foreign reserves. A 20-year-old has known nothing but upward mobility. Today, success has become a secular religion, reinforced by messages of opportunity in nearly every official speech—"sermons about paradise," as one Western scholar put it.

9   In some ways, China's money culture is spawning more avaricious—and unchecked—competition. There is a more intense game of keeping up with the Chans, but with no cushions like Rotary clubs, or other civil or volunteer structures. Some 40 percent of wealth is controlled by 10 percent. Young people are getting diplomas in record numbers, but unemployment is 10 percent for those under 30. "Underemployment" is far higher.

10   "The gap between expectations and salary continues to grow, and psychologically a great number of Chinese feel under more pressure," says Victor *Yuan*, director of Horizon Market Research in Beijing. "Expectations are high, but so are mortgages. The society is more consumerist, and many people are under heavy family pressure to satisfy demands. Some find it hard to maintain their jobs, let alone talk about expectations."

11   Ma Jinliu, who speaks perfect English, got a graduate degree at a European university. But he came home to the same job at a German joint venture he left two years earlier. "I didn't have a choice. The market is very tough... and I can't take my money from the housing fund, which is irritating."

12   An expectation crisis is less felt among the 3 percent of wealthy urban Chinese who hire drivers, send children to schools overseas, and make more than $1,200 a month. Rather, it is felt in a vastly broader category of urban Chinese who live in the new money culture, but don't yet have a firm stake in it. They earn between $150 to $350 per month—typical for civil servants, academics, clerks, military officers, engineers, and teachers. Good houses and cars

are hard to swing. On TV, they see others doing things they can't afford. Instead, they sock away savings for health care, knowing the system is not serving them well. Many feel cynical about the housing fund as they feel it will be years before they can use it. (Many marriages now involve "sharing expenses" as a principal motivator, one young person points out.)

13   Last month, the state decided not to increase wages 25 percent for this class—since it would widen the gap too far with earners just below that level. As one party member put it, "We all have expectations now. But I haven't reached them and I'm now in my 40s. I'm getting a little worried."

14   Many Chinese have strong principles of fair and unfair, right and wrong. They see people getting ahead by cutting corners or corruption. One colonel who makes $500 a month will not be promoted further; he will lose his car privilege, and it will be difficult to send his daughter to a top college. He feels he is losing out because he won't accept illegal side jobs.

(Words: 986)

Exercise I Discussion

Directions: Please discuss the following questions in pairs or groups.

1. Do you think this "keep up with the Chans" attitude is totally a negative phenomenon?
2. In what way can we effectively deal with social problems mentioned in the article?
3. What is a harmonious society in your mind?

Exercise II Writing

Directions: Do you think foreign media reflect the reality in China? Are they objective or subjective? Write a composition commenting on reports of foreign media about China in about 150 words.

UNIT FOUR

GREAT BRITAIN TODAY

Target of the Unit

☞ To get a glimpse of the modern British society
☞ To practice reading skills
☞ To enlarge your vocabulary

1) LEAD IN

Directions: In this unit, you will read 3 passages about what is happening in Great Britain. Read them and try to compare what is mentioned in the passages and the image of Great Britain in your mind.

2) DISCUSSION

Great Britain and the US are two major English-speaking countries. They were closely related to each other in history, but now they're very different. Can you think of some similarities and differences between the two countries from the cultural perspective?

Text A

Is Britain Still Home of Mannerly Charm? Don't be Daft!

By Mark Rice-Oxley

Warming-up Exercises

☞ How much do you know about Great Britain? How about the British people?

· First reading ·

Directions: Now please read the following passage as fast as you can and summarize the main idea.

1   LONDON—When Mark Duckworth started working at grocery stores in the late 1980s, customers still uttered **pleasantries** like "good morning," "please," and "thank you."

2   Sixteen years later, shoppers use a rather different lexicon. There are **muttered** insults, impatient outbursts, and all manner of curses not fit for print. Some even resort to physical abuse, like spitting, shoving, or punching.

> **pleasantry** *n.* things that you say to someone in order to be polite, but which are not very important 客套话，寒暄
> **mutter** *v.* grumble in an indistinct voice 咕哝着抱怨

3   "I was getting abuse every day," says Mr. Duckworth, who left his job due to a knee injury inflicted by a would-be shoplifter. Customers are "getting ruder and ruder," he adds. "The level of respect in society has just gone."

4   Duckworth is not alone. From doctors to train drivers, teachers to call-center staff, millions of British workers face rising levels of anger, impatience, and discourtesy from the public they serve.

5   Whatever happened to the mannerly isle full of polite souls who ask about each other's health over a cup of tea? Some observers say Britain has grown vulgar only in recent years. Others say things were never so genteel.

6   "There has been a gradual coarsening of our society," says Dr. Colin Gill, a psychologist at Leeds University. "Having said that, elements of society have always been incredibly coarse in this country; and it's just becoming more obvious now because the media actually tend to celebrate it."

7   Evidence of what the media have started calling "rude Britain" is everywhere, from surly service to road rage, noisy neighbors to cellphone selfishness.

8   A sales clerk in Britain is physically or verbally abused every minute, union officials charge.

In schools, thousands of teachers are **rebuked**, threatened, or assaulted by parents every year.

> **rebuke** *v.* reprimand, reprove 责骂，责备
> **brawling** *adj.* making a noisy quarrel or fight 大吵大闹的
> **connotation** *n.* to suggest or imply in addition to literal meaning 含义
> **lout** *n.* a very rude and violent person 举止粗鲁的人
> **absolutism** *n.* a political theory holding that all power should be vested in one ruler or other authority; a form of government in which all power is vested in a single ruler or other authority; an absolute doctrine, principle, or standard 绝对主义，专制主义

9   On Saturday nights, town centers are often a no-go area of **brawling** youths. At a soccer match last weekend, two stars were sent off for fighting—and they were on the same team.

10   On public transport, signs warn of punishment for anyone who physically assaults staff. Remarkably, casualty wards in hospitals carry the same signs, a clear indication that even the sick and wounded are losing their temper these days.

11   The trend is even taking on political **connotations** in the run-up to the May 5 general election, called Tuesday by Prime Minister Tony Blair. The government has tried to crack down on offensive behavior with a new on-the-spot order called an Asbo (antisocial behavior order). Opposition Conservatives have hit back, saying the government isn't doing enough and that they would be tougher on **louts** and boors.

12   The media has joined the debate with disapproving noises about "yob culture," though Dr. Gill argues that they may be part of the problem, given the tabloid tendency to champion the vulgar. With uncouth soccer stars and reality-TV contestants as role models, society has recalibrated its moral compass.

13   "The heroes of the modern generation have generally not embraced the traditional virtues," he notes.

14   But there are more fundamental reasons for "rude Britain" than that—reasons that have also led to a coarsening in other Western countries in recent years. Dr. Gill points to the death of moral **absolutism** as a major factor. "We have replaced 'thou shalt' and 'thou shalt not' with 'it's really up to you,'" he says.

15   Simon Fanshawe, whose book on etiquette and manners, *The Done Thing* is to be published this summer, agrees, noting that the deference and class-based model that used to enforce good behavior in Britain is a thing of the past.

16   "Manners used to be enforced through fear and deference to the Maker, the monarch, and the men," he says. "Now there is no longer a consensus that any of those three are an acceptable authority."

17   Instead, a culture of personal and economic freedom has grown up out of the sexual

revolution of the 1960s and the free-market revolution of the 1980s.

18   "Manners are a bargain between personal freedom and collective good," says Fanshawe. "We discovered personal freedom, and if an individual is always going for what he wants it will not always be what anyone else wants."

> **archetypal** adj. archetypical, typical, classic 典型的
> **irascible** adj. hot-tempered 脾气暴躁的
> **querulous** adj. complaining about things in an annoying way 爱抱怨的，爱发牢骚的
> **contrarian** n. one who takes a contrary view or action, especially an investor who makes decisions that contradict prevailing wisdom, as in buying securities that are unpopular at the time 唱反调的人，唱对台戏的人

19   Ian Gregory, who founded the Campaign for Courtesy, says the problem stems partly from the impatient quest for the "good life," which is presented by the media as attainable to everyone but which is actually enjoyed by very few. The result is frustration at failure to live up to unreasonable expectations.

20   "Nobody puts up with anything now," he says. "They push and shove to get their good life and people get hurt. We have become extremely acquisitive in a way our forebears never were."

21   Yet Fanshawe, Gregory, and others warn against excessive nostalgia. Graffiti, soccer hooliganism, and street brawling all date back decades, if not generations.

22   Indeed, some point out that Britain has a long history of brusque and occasional brutish behavior.

23   "In Victorian days, people could be raising their hat with one hand and picking your pocket with the other—there was a lot of hypocrisy about it," says Gregory.

24   A century earlier, the symbol of the **archetypal** Englishman was John Bull, a character portrayed as **irascible**, strong-minded, **querulous**, and not particularly neighborly. In cartoons he was soon depicted as a bulldog, hardly the most affable of creatures.

25   In the 17th century, historians note, there were two civil wars and one king decapitated. And Shakespeare's England was full of **contrarian** characters quick to rebuke their fellows with brutal put-downs.

26   Instead of looking misty-eyed to the past, Fanshawe urges a new code of conduct based on mutual respect, not on the fear and deference that prevailed in the past.

27   "The excitement is to be in a position where we can make new rules," he says.

28   Dr. Gill says this will be difficult. "There is virtually no moral code that is generally agreed and accepted across society," he says. "If we attempt to do so rationally, we immediately end up having arguments about why a particular view is the right one."

(Words: 998)

Second Reading

Directions: Read the text again more carefully to find enough information for Exercises I, II & III.

Exercise I   True or False

Directions: Please state whether the following statements are true or not (T/F) according to the text.

1. According to Mark Duckworth, we're living in a less polite society than 16 years ago.
2. The media are to blame for the coarsening of the country.
3. Teachers in Britain are not only assaulted by the students, but also by their parents.
4. Mr. Duckworth quit his job because he didn't want to be confronted by shoplifters any longer.
5. Great Britain used to be a very polite country, and it is only in recent years that Britain has grown vulgar.
6. Town centers should be avoided in Britain by the youths.
7. Some other Western countries became ruder due to the same reason as that of Britain.
8. Sexual revolution of the 1980s and the free-market revolution of the 1960s led to a culture of personal and economic freedom.
9. People in Britain become less patient because they have unreasonably high expectations.
10. According to Dr. Gill, it is irrational to work out some moral code that can be accepted across the country.

Exercise II   Word Inference

Directions: Often you can guess the meaning of a word/expression by reading the words around it. Please read the given sentence to see how each word/expression in bold type is used in the text. Then choose the answer that is closest in meaning to the bold-faced word/expression.

1. Is Britain still home of mannerly charm? Don't be **daft**!
   A. silly   B. impolite
   C. sure   D. happy

2. …millions of British workers face rising levels of anger, impatience, and **discourtesy** from the public they serve.

   A. anger

   B. temper

   C. polite behavior

   D. impolite behavior

3. Some observers say Britain has grown **vulgar** only in recent years.

   A. uncouth   B. stout

   C. harassing   D. annoying

4. Evidence of what the media have started calling "rude Britain" is everywhere, from **surly** service to road rage…

   A. hard   B. rude

   C. legal   D. personal

5. Opposition Conservatives have hit back, saying the government isn't doing enough and that they would be tougher on louts and **boors**.

   A. rude persons

   B. beggars

   C. juvenile delinquents

   D. mobs

6. The media has joined the debate with disapproving noises about "**yob** culture"…

   A. popular   B. ruffian

   C. lout   D. mass

7. With uncouth soccer stars and reality-TV contestants as role models, society has **recalibrated** its moral compass.

   A. re-done   B. reworked

   C. re-adjusted   D. re-made

8. We have become extremely **acquisitive** in a way our forebears never were.

   A. greedy   B. curious

   C. obscene   D. violent

9. Yet Fanshawe, Gregory, and others warn against excessive **nostalgia**.

   A. gloom   B. reflection

   C. homesickness   D. eagerness

10. In cartoons he was soon depicted as a bulldog, hardly the most **affable** of creatures.

    A. friendly   B. rude

    C. persevering   D. fussy

> **Exercise III   Discussion**
> *Directions: Please discuss the following questions in pairs or groups.*

1. Do you agree that manners are a bargain between personal freedom and collective good?
2. What's your suggestion to solve the problem mentioned in the text?

Text B

Saving the Day

By Monika Queisser, Edward Whitehouse and Peter Whiteford

Warming-up Exercises

☞ What do you know about China's pension system?

• First reading •

Directions: Now please read the following passage as fast as you can and summarize the main idea.

1   ___A___. Just how **stingy** it is emerges from a report this week from the OECD: the promise made to today's young workers is the least generous in the developed world.

> **stingy** *adj.* spending, using unwillingly 吝啬的，不大方的
> **compulsory** *adj.* obligatory; required 强制的
> **thereabouts** *n.* near a particular time, place, number etc, but not exactly 大约，左右，上下

2   Monika Queisser and Edward Whitehouse, the report's authors, estimate what those who are young today will get from the state and **compulsory** private-pension schemes when they hang up their boots in 2050 or **thereabouts**. Average earners in Britain can expect a pension worth just 31% of what they are earning before they retire, compared with 41% in America, 68% in Italy and 96% in Greece. ___B___.

3   ___C___. Greece's pension promise is too good to be true, since it would impose an

unbearable burden on future taxpayers. Britain's may look **affordable** but it is politically unsustainable, since it would **consign** future pensioners to an unacceptably low standard of living if they were to rely upon the state.

> **affordable** *adj.* that can be afforded 可以承受的，可以（买）得起的
> **consign** *v.* hand over, give up 移交，交付
> **inadequacy** *n.* a weakness or failing 弱点，不足

4 The report underlines why reforms now going through Britain's Parliament are essential. The age when people become eligible to receive state pensions will rise from 65 in the early 2020s to 68 by the mid-2040s. And the basic state pension will be re-linked in 2012 to earnings, which increase faster than prices. The OECD's calculations assume the second reform is already in place, but not the first.

5 Another change is also vital if young workers are to look forward to a decent retirement, for many of the corporate final-salary pension schemes, which did much to make up for the **inadequacies** of the state system, are now closed to new members. __D__.

6 The idea is to enroll in these new accounts most employees who are not already members of a pension plan in which the employer contributes at least 3% of a worker's pay. Around 10m people, mainly low-to-moderate earners, are likely to fall into this category. Although they will be enrolled automatically, they are free to leave the scheme if they choose. Employers will contribute 3% of a worker's eligible earnings (now £5,000—£35,000) and employees 4%. Tax relief will add another 1%, making a total contribution rate of 8%. The government put its proposals out for consultation in December and is due to respond to comments next week.

7 The OECD's calculations suggest that the new accounts could do the trick. With a total contribution rate of 7% on all pay, an average earner's pension would rise from 31% of pre-retirement pay to the OECD mean of 59%. But this encouraging finding assumes that workers contribute throughout their 45-year careers. If they started ten years later—at 30 rather than 20—they would need to save nearly 10% of their pay. The government's own forecasts, which take likely interruptions into account by assuming continuous, saving from age 30, suggest that the new accounts will give

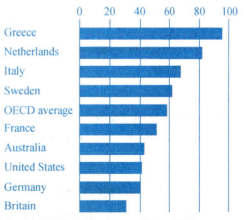

Poor promise
Mandatory pension as % of pay for average earners retiring around 2050

Greece
Netherlands
Italy
Sweden
OECD average
France
Australia
United States
Germany
Britain

Source: OECD, *Pensions at a Glance* 2007

median earners a pension worth around 45% of their pay before retirement.

8   Britain, with New Zealand, is breaking new ground in introducing a retirement-saving plan using the device of automatic enrolment. __E__. The OECD research suggests that there will have to be a lot of successful nudging, however, if young workers are to have a hope of securing a reasonable pension.

> **median** *n.* It is one type of average, found by arranging the values in order and then selecting the one in the middle. If the total number of values in the sample is even, then the median is the mean of the two middle numbers. The median is a useful number in cases where the distribution has very large extreme values which would otherwise skew the data 中项，中位数

(Words: 591)

• Second Reading •

Directions: Read the text again more carefully to find enough information for Exercises I, II, III, IV & V.

Exercise I Understanding Text Organization

Directions: You may find there are a few sentences (segments) missing from the passage. Read the article through and decide where the following sentences should go.

1. The government wants to introduce, also in 2012, a new system of personal retirement-saving accounts.
2. The average across all 30 OECD countries is 59% (see chart).
3. The reform dodges the thorn of compulsion by nudging people towards the desired course of action.
4. Britain's state-pension system is known to be tight-fisted.
5. This is an inter-generational game where neither a low nor a top score is cause to celebrate.

Exercise II Multiple-Choice Questions

Directions: Please choose the best answer from the four choices given.

1. According to OECD, the promise made to today's young workers in Great Britain ranks _____ in the developed world.
   A. the first

B. the last

C. the second

D. the last but one

2. In Great Britain, the mandatory pension is worth _____ of pay for average earners retiring around 2050.

   A. 96%

   B. 59%

   C. 41%

   D. 31%

3. Why is Greece's pension promise too good to be true?

   A. Because it will not be affordable financially.

   B. Because it will not be sustainable politically.

   C. Because it will be affordable financially.

   D. Because it will be sustainable politically.

4. Why is the enrolment of those who are not already members of a pension plan vital to many young workers?

   A. Because millions of them will fall into this category.

   B. Because they are free to leave the scheme if they choose.

   C. Because they can get a total contribution rate of 4%.

   D. Because it will be passed in December.

5. The government's own forecasts suggest that the new accounts will give median earners a pension worth around _____ of their pay before retirement.

   A. 59%

   B. 45%

   C. 49%

   D. 55%

Exercise III Word Matching

Directions: Please choose from among the supplied words to explain the original forms of the boldfaced words in the following sentences.

A. stingy   B. pushing   C. avoid   D. to be in the right age   E. force

1. Greece's pension promise is too good to be true, since it would **impose** an unbearable burden on future taxpayers.

2. The reform **dodges** the thorn of compulsion by nudging people towards the desired

course of action.

3. The age when people become **eligible** to receive state pensions will rise from 65 in the early 2020s to 68 by the mid-2040s.
4. Britain's state-pension system is known to be **tight-fisted**.
5. The OECD research suggests that there will have to be a lot of successful **nudging**, however, if young workers are to have a hope of securing a reasonable pension.

Exercise IV   Short-Answer Questions

Directions: Please answer the following questions briefly in your own words.

1. Why does the author say it is an inter-generational game?
2. What does automatic enrolment mean?

Exercise V   Discussion

Directions: Please discuss the following questions in pairs or groups.

1. In your opinion, who should pay for the employees' retirement pension?
2. What do you think of a welfare state?

Text C

Come and Fall on Slough

By Unnamed Author

1   Plumbers, or a lack of them, were one reason for the warm welcome Britain gave the eight eastern European nations that joined the EU in 2004. A few thousand skilled migrants seemed exactly what the economy needed. Officials sat back and awaited the new arrivals—about 30,000 or so, they assumed. Two years later, some 600,000 eager migrants had turned up, providing more than enough handymen for a small island. Now the government is more cautious. Romanians and Bulgarians, whose countries joined the EU in January, may enter Britain freely, but they are not allowed to work or claim state support.

2   Plenty are coming anyway. Slough, a smallish town on the outskirts of London, says that about 400 Romanian Roma (or gypsies) have moved in since January 1st. (No one is quite sure why they have chosen Slough; they may know the small group of Romanian refugees who settled there around 2000.) Banned from working or claiming benefits, the newcomers are thought to be making a living through trading, odd jobs, begging and some petty crime. The council says multiple families are cramming into cheap rented rooms in order to save money. The rage of some British newspapers is matched only by Romania's, which fears (sadly, correctly) that the Roma are giving their country a bad name.

3   This week it emerged that 88 of Slough's Roma are unaccompanied minors. The young migrants came in small sibling groups, travelling in the backs of lorries for €75 (£51) apiece. Six had babies of their own, and seven were pregnant.

4   Lone minors of any nationality are entitled to a bed, a £45 ($89) weekly food allowance, a one-off £100 clothing grant, health care and, if they are under 16, free schooling. Perversely, being accompanied by an adult would immediately deprive them of these benefits. Slough is trying to reunite its newcomers with their families in Romania, but without much luck. Instead, 35 have been sent to live with relatives in Britain. The rest are with foster families or in hostels. So far, supporting these young arrivals has cost Slough £150,000.

5   Few councils suffer such crises, but many are unhappy at what they see as the unrecognised burden that immigration imposes on them. Official statistics on EU migration are shaky, partly because many newcomers are self-employed and don't register as workers, and partly because departures often are not recorded. Last month a new official approach to counting heads claimed that some areas had fewer migrants than was previously thought.

6   This is explosive stuff, since the size of a council's grant from central government is partly based on population. Resentful locals already say that immigrants stretch their services and increase their taxes. Westminster council, in central London, reckons it will now lose £6m a year because its officially recognised migrants may fall by 15,500. Three other nearby councils have made the same complaint.

7   Landing strips such as London probably scored disproportionately highly under the old way of counting immigrants, says John Salt of University College London. This relied on

census data and a survey of international passengers' intentions. "A lot of people first say they are going to London, but we know that quite a lot of them later move on," says Mr. Salt.

8   The new method takes in the Labour Force Survey, a house-to-house questionnaire, to give a better idea of who has moved where since touching down. It is expected to show that six of the ten biggest drops will be in and around the capital, whereas smaller cities will see increases.

9   Unfair, say the losers. The new approach does not include anyone planning to stay in Britain for less than a year, meaning that transit points such as London probably have many unrecorded new inhabitants. (Someone who is around for 11 months will still use plenty of local services, councils point out.) And household surveys are a bad way to poll new migrants, since they exclude anyone who lives in a hostel, works awkward hours or isn't confident in English.

10 Councils are compiling their own rival statistics. Slough says it has seen a sharp rise in national-insurance applications, for example. And to prove how busy the town has become, the council even measured local sewage flow: in the year to April 2006 it swelled by more than 10%.

(Words: 725)

Exercise I Discussion
Directions: Please discuss the following questions in pairs or groups.

1. What are the benefits and threats to the countries involved in regional integration?
2. Do you think immigration or emigration might be a problem for China in the near future? How about migration within the country?

Exercise II Writing
Directions: Write a composition in about 150 words, stating the benefits of accepting migrant workers into metropolitan areas based on the research you've done.

UNIT FIVE

THE CHANGING AMERICAN CULTURE

Target of the Unit

☞ To get a glimpse of the changing American culture
☞ To practice reading skills
☞ To enlarge your vocabulary

1) LEAD IN

Directions: In this unit, you will read 3 passages about American culture. Read them and get a glimpse of the changes that have happened to it.

2) DISCUSSION

How much do you know about American culture? What is the influence of American culture on the world today?

Text A

Demand Growing for Taller Christmas Trees

By Holly Ramer

Warming-up Exercises

☞ What do you know about Christmas? And how do you like the idea of putting a tree in your house during the Christmas holiday?

· First reading ·

Directions: Now please read the following passage as fast as you can and summarize the main idea.

61

1   Taller Christmas trees are in demand this holiday season, but some buyers' eyes are bigger than their living rooms.

2   While some families are looking for larger trees to fill **cavernous**, cathedral-ceilinged "great rooms" in their upscale homes, others simply want the biggest and best product, even if that means the tree trimming starts with **chopping** a foot or more off the trunk when they discover it won't fit in their home.

> **cavernous** *adj.* resembling a cavern, as in depth, vastness, or effect 在深度、广度或效果上类似洞穴的；瓮音的，瓮声瓮气
> **chop** *v.* cut, hack, fell 砍伐
> **condominium** *n.* one apartment in a building with several apartments, each of which is owned by the people living in it 一套公寓房间，一个住宅单元

3   "I've never gone home with anyone to find out, but I think it's human nature to go bigger," said David Murray of Murray Farms Greenhouse in Concord, who sells trees up to 13 feet tall. "When you're outdoors, a tree certainly has a different look than it does in a living room."

4   Murray advertises that his trees are "extra thick, extra tall, for that extra big room!" But he and others in the industry say that for every customer with a large room to fill, there's another with unrealistic visions dancing in their heads.

5   "It's like people buying an enormous roast of beef and only eating half of it and then feeding the rest to the dog," said Steve Taylor, New Hampshire's agriculture commissioner. "It's a function of our affluent society."

6   New Hampshire has more than 300 Christmas tree growers, though only about 50 have large commercial operations.

7   The National Christmas Tree Association doesn't keep statistics on the size of trees, though it did commission a survey several years ago asking consumers whether the height of their trees had increased, decreased or stayed the same over the last five years. The responses were evenly split among the three options, but spokesman Rick Dungey said he has heard anecdotal accounts of strong consumer interest in taller trees.

8   Irwin Loiterstein, a Christmas tree wholesaler in St. Louis, serves on the association's board of directors and works with growers nationwide. He said tall trees are in demand, but so are tiny ones suited to apartments and **condominiums**.

9   "There's been big surge in smaller and taller trees," he said. "I had a bunch of them last week and got rid of them, and all of a sudden I'm getting calls all over the place."

10   In Bedford, Katie Moore and her family put up their 10-foot tree on Sunday.

11   "We always get the biggest one that will fit in the biggest room we have," she said.

ornament *n.* decoration, embellishment 装饰物
swag *n.* an ornamental festoon 悬垂饰

12   Other than the year when the tree had a bent trunk and had to be wired to the wall, Moore said she generally has had good luck finding tall trees. Getting them home and decorated also hasn't been too difficult.

13   "I have a lot of **ornaments**, and I buy new ones every year," she said. "But the lights can be a challenge."

14   For those who find that their ceilings are too low to accommodate the huge trees they lug home, Taylor offers some advice: use the surplus branches to make other decorations.

15   "Some people make **swags**," he said.

(Words: 510)

• Second Reading •

Directions: Read the text again more carefully to find enough information for Exercises I, II & III.

Exercise I True or False

Directions: Please state whether the following statements are true or false (T/F) according to what you've found in the text.

1. Americans love taller Christmas trees because they all have big houses.
2. Nowadays, many people would buy an enormous roast of beef and only eat half of it.
3. Americans usually get Christmas trees by chopping down trees in the forests.
4. According to the statistics kept by the National Christmas Tree Association, Americans have strong interest in taller Christmas trees.
5. As the demand for tall trees is growing, tiny ones are no longer wanted by people.
6. Some people who buy taller trees will have to cut them shorter to fit them into their houses.
7. If people buy too tall trees, they can cut them short and make use of the cut branches.

8. Americans seem to love bigger things.

9. Many people who buy taller Christmas trees are in fact unrealistic.

10. It seems that only half of those buy taller trees do have large enough rooms to accommodate them.

> **Exercise II Word Inference**
>
> *Directions: Often you can guess the meaning of a word/expression by reading the words around it. Please read the given sentence to see how each word/expression in bold type is used in the text. Then choose the answer that is closest in meaning to the bold-faced word/expression.*

1. While some families are looking for larger trees to fill cavernous, cathedral-ceilinged "great rooms" in their **upscale** homes…

    A. large

    B. tall

    C. old

    D. upper-class

2. …others simply want the biggest and best product, even if that means the tree **trimming** starts with chopping a foot or more off the trunk when they discover it won't fit in their home.

    A. cutting

    B. decorating

    C. reducing

    D. moving

3. But he and others in the industry say that for every customer with a large room to fill, there's another with unrealistic **visions** dancing in their heads.

    A. sight

    B. foresight

    C. things seen vividly in the imagination

    D. pictures

4. It's a **function** of our affluent society.

    A. the job that someone or something does

    B. feature

    C. weakness

    D. the purpose that something has

5. It's a function of our **affluent** society.

   A. vain
   B. wealthy
   C. crazy
   D. superficial

6. The National Christmas Tree Association doesn't keep statistics on the size of trees, though it did **commission** a survey several years ago…

   A. finish
   B. give sb the task to do sth
   C. sponsor
   D. conclude

7. The responses were evenly split among the three options, but spokesman Rick Dungey said he has heard **anecdotal** accounts of strong consumer interest in taller trees.

   A. legendary
   B. official
   C. stories-based
   D. reliable

8. There's been big **surge** in smaller and taller trees.

   A. tide
   B. sudden increase
   C. popularity
   D. demand

9. For those who find that their ceilings are too low to **accommodate** the huge trees they lug home…

   A. hold
   B. cover
   C. maintain
   D. sustain

10. …Taylor offers some advice: use the **surplus** branches to make other decorations.

    A. more than is needed
    B. bigger than is needed
    C. harder than is needed
    D. smaller than is needed

Exercise III Discussion

Directions: Please discuss the following questions in pairs or groups.

1. Why do Americans love bigger things? Are bigger things always better?
2. What effect the custom of keeping big Christmas trees at home may have on the environment?

Text B

Storm Changed Americans' Attitudes

By Erin McClam

Warming-up Exercises

☞ Have you ever heard of Hurricane Katrina?
☞ How do you think it might have affected the United States?

• First reading •

Directions: Now please read the following passage as fast as you can and summarize the main idea.

1   A 64-year-old Alabamian **frets** about frayed race relations. A Utah software programmer ponders the slow government response to **Hurricane Katrina** and decides he'll turn to his church first in a disaster created by nature or terrorists.

2   A woman **scraping by** on disability pay in northern Virginia puts her house on the market because of surging post-storm gas and food prices. Cheaper to live in Pennsylvania, she figures.

> **fret** *v.* worry, vex 着急，不安
> **Hurricane Katrina** *n.* Occurring in 2005, it was the costliest hurricane of the Atlantic hurricane season, as well as one of the five deadliest, in the history of the United States 飓风卡特里娜
> **scrape by** *v.phr.* have just enough money to live 勉强糊口
> **swirl** *v.* to move with a twisting or whirling motion 旋转

3   As the Gulf Coast braces for another monster storm, a new Associated Press-Ipsos poll shows Katrina prompted a rethinking of some signature issues in American life—changing the way we view race and our safety, how we spend our money, even where we live.

4   The poll shows that issues **swirling** around Katrina trump other national concerns.

5   Asked to rank eight topics that should be priorities for President Bush and Congress, respondents placed the economy, gas prices and Iraq high.   __A__.

6   Like bands of the storm itself, Katrina's reach in American life is vast: 1 in 3 Americans believes the slow response will harm race relations. Two-thirds say surging gas prices will cause hardship for their families. Half say the same of higher food

prices.

7   In Las Cruces, N.M., Ariana Darley relies on carpools to get to parenting classes, or to make doctor's appointments with her 1-year-old son, Jesse. Before, she **chipped in** $5 for gas. Now, she pays $10 to $15.

> **chip in** v. phr. Each gives a small amount of money so that they can do sth together 凑钱，凑份子
> **huddle** v. crowd together 挤到一块儿
> **fabric** n. structure, framework 结构
> **literal** adj. factual 实际的
> **respondent** n. one who responds 回答者

8   "I didn't think it would affect me," she says by telephone, with Jesse crying in the background. "But it costs a lot of money now. I have to go places, and now it adds up."

9   After a crisis with indisputable elements of race and class—searing images of mostly poor, mostly black New Orleans residents **huddled** on rooftops or waiting in lines for buses—some Americans worry about strains in the nation's social **fabric**.

10   ___B___. One of them is Sue Hubbard of Hueytown, Ala., 64 years old. She does not believe race played a deliberate part in who got out of New Orleans, but she is deeply worried about tensions inflamed by those who do.

11   "I just think it took everybody by surprise," says Hubbard, who is white. "I don't care if it would have been the president himself, they couldn't have gotten there to those people. Some people—not everybody—are trying to make a racist thing out of it."

12   The poll underscores the **literal** reach of Katrina as well: 55 percent of Americans say evacuees from Katrina have turned up in their cities or communities, raising concerns about living conditions for the refugees, vanishing jobs for locals and—among 1 in 4 **respondents**—increased crime.

13   Among respondents with incomes under $25,000 per year, 56 percent were concerned about living conditions for refugees in shelters; that was higher than among those who make

more money. And the poll indicates people in the South, which has absorbed huge masses of evacuees, are most concerned about the costs to their local governments.

> **aftermath** *n.* a consequence, especially of a disaster or misfortune 严重后果
> **spasm** *n.* a sudden, involuntary contraction of a muscle or group of muscles 痉挛，抽搐
> **esophagus** *n.* the tube that connects the pharynx (throat) with the stomach 食道

14　　Ann McMullen, 52, of Killeen, Texas, who works as a school administrator at Fort Hood, says she worries about gang violence, simply because of the prodigious numbers of people flowing into Texas communities.

15　　"They can't even locate the sex offenders," she says. "And every population has gang members. It's theft, it's murder, it's more chaotic crimes in the community. Hopefully we'll be able to put these people back to work."

16　　 C   . Half say the government should give people in those zones money for recovery, but almost as many say those people should live there at their own risk.

17　　About 4 in 10 say the government should prohibit people from building new homes in those endangered areas in the first place. As McMullen puts it: "You're asking for another disaster to happen."

18　　Katrina has also raised grave doubts among Americans about just who will protect them in the **aftermath** of a natural disaster or a terrorist attack.

19　　Only about a quarter of Americans believe the federal government was as prepared as it should have been to cope with a disaster of Katrina's magnitude.   D   .

20　　Reed Chadwick, a 33-year-old software programmer from Herriman, Utah, has made a mental list of the organizations he can count on should Mother Nature or terrorists strike—church first, then local government, then the feds.

21　　"I think a lot of people have been yelling at Bush," he says. "But I think they're not looking at their local leaders for answers or reasons why things did or did not work. A lot of people are asking questions."

22　　As for other personal effects of the storm, rising gas prices have not been crippling for his household yet, he says. "But I know it's going to put a dent into my budget. I won't be able to do dinner as much, maybe take only one vacation, if that."

23　　For Pam Koren, the storm's impact has been more immediate—and more drastic.

24　　Suffering from low blood sugar, **spasms** of the **esophagus** and nerve damage, she exists now on disability pay and contributions from her daughter, who attends college and works as an assistant youth minister.

25　　With gas and food prices rising after the storm, she says, she was forced to put her house in Burke, Va., on the market. She is considering east-central Pennsylvania, and a less expensive home.

26 "I'm a wreck because I'm not sure I'm making the right decision," she says. "I didn't want to have to do this, but things have become so tight I have not had a choice. I did not expect things were going to get this bad."

27 ___E___.

(Words: 1006)

Second Reading

Directions: Read the text again more carefully to find enough information for Exercises I, II, III, IV & V.

Exercise I Understanding Text Organization

Directions: You may find there are a few sentences (segments) missing from the passage. Read the article through and decide where the following sentences should go.

1. Women were especially concerned.
2. Only slightly more than half, 54 percent, are confident in the federal government's ability to handle a future major disaster.
3. But when Katrina recovery was added to the list, it swamped everything else.
4. The poll of 1,000 adults conducted by Ipsos, an international polling company, had a margin of potential sampling error of plus or minus 3 percentage points.
5. The poll also exposes a divide among Americans in how the government should respond when disasters strike areas particularly prone to catastrophe—landslides, earthquakes, hurricanes.

Exercise II Multiple-Choice Questions

Directions: Complete each of the following statements with the best choice given.

1. According to the mentioned poll, Katrina has changed _____.
   A. the way Americans view race relations
   B. the way Americans spend their money
   C. the way Americans view their safety

D. all the above

2. The poll shows that Americans thought _____ should be the first priority for President Bush.

   A. Iraq

   B. economy

   C. Katrina recovery

   D. gas prices

3. The storm victims who suffered the most were very likely to be _____.

   A. poor whites

   B. poor blacks

   C. poor Native Americans

   D. poor Asian-Americans

4. The influx of huge masses of refugees from New Orleans has raised concerns about _____ in neighboring cities and communities.

   A. surging gas prices

   B. higher food prices

   C. danger of an epidemic

   D. increased crime

5. _____ percent of respondents have doubts about the federal government's ability to handle a future major disasters.

   A. 46

   B. 25

   C. 54

   D. 50

Exercise III Word Matching

Directions: Please choose from among the supplied words to explain the original forms of the boldfaced words in the following sentences.

A. disturbing   B. emphasize   C. strained   D. large   E. beat

1. A 64-year-old Alabamian frets about **frayed** race relations.

2. The poll shows that issues swirling around Katrina **trump** other national concerns.

3. After a crisis with indisputable elements of race and class—**searing** images of mostly poor, mostly black New Orleans residents huddled on rooftops or waiting in lines for

buses….

4. The poll **underscores** the literal reach of Katrina as well.
5. … says she worries about gang violence, simply because of the **prodigious** numbers of people flowing into Texas communities.

Exercise IV Short-Answer Questions

Directions: Please answer the following questions briefly in your own words.

1. Why the crisis is described as one "with indisputable elements of race and class"?
2. What kind of a divide among Americans was exposed by the poll?
3. What organizations might many Americans turn to for help in time of a major disaster?

Exercise V Discussion

1. How could the storm have changed Americans' attitudes so much? What else might also be held responsible for such a change?
2. How do you explain the fact that poorer people were more concerned about living conditions for refugees in shelters than those who are richer?

Text C

How to Tell if You're American?

By Web blog contributors

1   Not long ago, one of those earnest-freshman puppydogs on the Net declared that there was "no such thing as American culture." Right. Fish have also been known to doubt the existence of water.

2   The following is a first crack at an ostensive definition of "American culture"—things shared by the vast majority (let's say 90%) of native-born Americans. Many of these won't sound "cultural" at all to Americans; they'll sound like just descriptions of the way things are. But each one of them would be contested in one or more non-American cultures.

3   **If you're American...**

4   You believe deep down in the First Amendment, guaranteed by the government and perhaps by God.

5   You're familiar with David Letterman, Mary Tyler Moore, Saturday Night Live, Bewitched, the Flintstones, Sesame Street, Mr. Rogers, Bob Newhart, Bill Cosby, Bugs Bunny, Road Runner, Donald Duck, the Fonz, Archie Bunker, Star Trek, the Honeymooners, the Addams Family, the Three Stooges, and Beetle Bailey.

6   You know how baseball, basketball, and American football are played. If you're male, you can argue intricate points about their rules. On the other hand (and unless you're under about 20), you don't care that much for soccer.

7   You count yourself fortunate if you get three weeks of vacation a year.

8   **If you died tonight...**

9   You're fairly likely to believe in God; if not, you've certainly been approached by people asking whether you know that you're going to Heaven.

10   You think of McDonald's, Burger King, KFC etc. as cheap food.

11   You probably own a telephone and a TV. Your place is heated in the winter and has its own bathroom. You do your laundry in a machine. You don't kill your own food. You don't have a dirt floor. You eat at a table, sitting on chairs.

12   You don't consider insects, dogs, cats, monkeys, or guinea pigs to be food.

13   A bathroom may not have a bathtub in it, but it certainly has a toilet.

14   It seems natural to you that the telephone system, railroads, auto manufacturers, airlines, and power companies are privately run; indeed, you can hardly picture things working differently.

15   You expect, as a matter of course, that the phones will work. Getting a new phone is routine.

16   The train system, by contrast, isn't very good. Trains don't go any faster than cars; you're better off taking a plane.

17   You find a two-party system natural. You expect the politicians of both parties to be responsive to business, strong on defense, and concerned with the middle class. You find parliamentary systems (such as Italy's) inefficient and comic.

18   Between "black" and "white" there are no other races. Someone with one black and one white parent looks black to you.

19   You think most problems could be solved if only people would put aside their prejudices and work together.

20   You take a strong court system for granted, even if you don't use it. You know that if you

went into business and had problems with a customer, partner, or supplier, you could take them to court.

21   You'd respect someone who speaks French, German, or Japanese—but you very likely don't yourself speak them well enough to communicate with a monolingual foreigner. You're a bit more ambivalent about Spanish; you think the schools should teach kids English.

22   It's not all that necessary to learn foreign languages anyway. You can travel the continent using nothing but English—and get by pretty well in the rest of the world, too.

23   You think a tax level of 30% is scandalously high.

24   School is free through high school (at least, it's an option, even if you went to private school); college isn't, unless you get a scholarship.

25   College is (normally, and excluding graduate study) four years long.

26   **Everybody knows that**

27   Mustard comes in jars. Shaving cream comes in cans. Milk comes in plastic jugs or cardboard boxes, and occasionally in bottles.

28   The date comes second: 11/22/63. (And you know what happened on that date.)

29   The decimal point is a dot. Certainly not a comma.

30   A billion is a thousand times a million.

31   World War II was a just war, and (granted all the suffering of course) ended all right. It was a time when the country came together and did what was right. And instead of insisting on vengeance, the US very generously rebuilt Europe instead, with the Marshall Plan.

32   You expect marriages to be made for love, not arranged by third parties. Getting married by a judge is an option, but not a requirement; most marriages happen in church. You have a best man and a maid or matron of honor at the wedding—a friend or a sibling. And, naturally, a man gets only one wife at a time.

33   If a man has sex with another man, he's a homosexual.

34   Once you're introduced to someone (well, besides the President and other lofty figures), you can call them by their first name.

35   If you're a woman, you don't go to the beach topless.

36   A hotel room has a private bath.

37   You'd rather a film be subtitled than dubbed (if you go to foreign films at all).

38   You seriously expect to be able to transact business, or deal with the government, without paying bribes.

39   If a politician has been cheating on his wife, you would question his ability to govern.

40   Just about any store will take your credit card.

41   A company can fire just about anybody it wants, unless it discriminates by doing so.

42 You like your bacon crisp (unless it's Canadian bacon, of course).

43 Labor Day is in the fall.

44 **Contributions to world civilization**

45 You've probably seen *Star Wars, ET, Home Alone, Casablanca,* and *Snow White*. If you're under forty, add *Blazing Saddles, Terminator, Jaws,* and *2001;* otherwise, add *Gone with the Wind, A Night at the Opera, Psycho,* and *Citizen Kane*.

46 You know the Beatles, the Rolling Stones, Bob Dylan, Elvis, Chuck Berry, Michael Jackson, Simon & Garfunkel, Linda Ronstadt. If not, you know Frank Sinatra, Al Jolson, Duke Ellington, Louis Armstrong, Tony Bennett, and Kate Smith.

47 You count on excellent medical treatment. You know you're not going to die of cholera or other Third World diseases. You expect very strong measures to be taken to save very ill babies or people in their eighties. You think dying at 65 would be a tragedy.

48 You went over US history, and some European, in school, not much Russian, Chinese, or Latin American. You couldn't name ten US interventions in Latin America.

49 You expect the military to fight wars, not get involved in politics. You may not be able to name the head of the Joint Chiefs of Staff.

50 Your country has never been conquered by a foreign nation.

51 You're used to a wide variety of choices for almost anything you buy.

52 You still measure things in feet, pounds, and gallons.

53 You are not a farmer.

54 Comics basically come in two varieties: newspaper comics and magazines; the latter pretty much all feature superheroes.

55 The people who appear on the most popular talk shows are mostly entertainers, politicians, or rather strange individuals. Certainly not, say, authors.

56 You drive on the right side of the road. You stop at red lights even if nobody's around. If you're a pedestrian and cars are stopped at a red light, you will fearlessly cross the street in front of them.

57 You think of Canada as a pleasant, peaceful, but rather dull country, which has suddenly developed an inexplicable problem in Québec. You probably couldn't explain why the Canadians didn't join the other British colonies in rebelling against King George.

58 You consider the Volkswagen Beetle to be a small car.

59 The police are armed, but not with submachine guns.

60 If a woman is plumper than the average, it doesn't improve her looks.

61 The biggest meal of the day is in the evening.

62 The nationality people most often make jokes about is the Poles.

63   There's parts of the city you definitely want to avoid at night.

64   **Outside the Beltway**

65   You feel that your kind of people aren't being listened to enough in Washington.

66   You wouldn't expect both inflation and unemployment to be very high (say, over 15%) at the same time.

67   You don't care very much what family someone comes from.

68   The normal thing, when a couple dies, is for their estate to be divided equally between their children.

69   You think of opera and ballet as rather elite entertainments. It's likely you don't see that many plays, either.

70   Christmas is in the winter. Unless you're Jewish, you spend it with your family, give presents, and put up a tree.

71   You may think the church is too powerful, or the state is; but you are used to not having a state church and don't think that it would be a good idea.

72   You'd be hard pressed to name the capitals or the leaders of all the nations of Europe.

73   You *aren't* familiar with Mafalda, Lucky Luke, Corto Maltese, Milo Manara, Guido Crepax, Gotlib, or Moebius.

74   You've left a message at the beep.

75   Taxis are generally operated by foreigners, who are often deplorably ignorant about the city.

76   You are distrustful of welfare and unemployment payments—you think people should earn a living and not take handouts. But you would not be in favor of eliminating Social Security and Medicare.

77   If you want to be a doctor, you need to get a bachelor's first.

78   There sure are a lot of lawyers.

79   **Space and time**

80   If you have an appointment, you'll mutter an excuse if you're five minutes late, and apologize profusely if it's ten minutes. An hour late is almost inexcusable.

81   If you're talking to someone, you get uncomfortable if they approach closer than about two feet.

82   About the only things you expect to bargain for are houses, cars, and antiques. Haggling is largely a matter of finding the hidden point that's the buyer's minimum.

83   Once you're past college, you very rarely simply show up at someone's place. People have to invite each other over—especially if a meal is involved.

84   When you negotiate, you are polite, of course, but it's only good business to "play

hardball". Some foreigners pay excessive attention to status, or don't say what they mean, and that's exasperating.

If you have a business appointment or interview with someone, you expect to have that person to yourself, and the business shouldn't take more than an hour or so.

(Words: 1810)

Exercise I   Discussion

Directions: Please discuss the following questions in pairs or groups.

1. Do you think the characteristics listed here are typical of Americans at all?
2. Is what you've learned from the text any different from your earlier assumptions about the Americans? Please say something about your new observations.
3. In your opinion, what are the most admirable qualities in the Americans and what are the most disagreeable ones in them?

Exercise II   Writing

Directions: Write a composition in about 150 words, stating your opinion on the influence of Western festivals on the Chinese society.

UNIT SIX

COMMUNICATION AND INTERPERSONAL SKILLS

Target of the Unit

☞ To learn about how to communicate with others effectively without causing misunderstanding and hard feelings
☞ To practice reading skills
☞ To enlarge your vocabulary

1) LEAD IN

Directions: In this unit, you will read 3 passages about how to improve your communication with others. Read them and see whether you have more ideas to offer.

2) DISCUSSION

What is the importance of friendship in your life?

Text A

Maintain a Healthy Relationship with Your Parents

By Unnamed Author

Warming-up Exercises

☞ Do you think there is always such a "generation gap" between you and your parents? Why?

• First reading •

Directions: Now please read the following passage as fast as you can and summarize the main idea.

1 Of course you love your parents—that's a given. But at times, maintaining the bond between parent and adult child can be as challenging as that between parent and teenager.

2 These days, both of you are confronting new challenges—retirement or career changes, health issues, concerns about the future. It's to be expected these issues will affect your relationship, but as you change, so, too, must your relationship with your parents change.

> **mature** *adj.* of, relating to, or characteristic of full development, either mental or physical 身心成熟的
> **stealth** *n.* avoiding detection by moving carefully 秘密，鬼祟
> **cornerstone** *n.* the fundamental assumptions from which something is begun or developed or calculated or explained 基石

3 Part of that evolution requires forging a new relationship, one between **mature** adults rather than "parent" and "child." You already have the basic underpinnings—love and shared memories. Add mutual respect and common interests and you may find a more fulfilling relationship with your mother and your father than any you've had since childhood.

4 Of course, some things never change—Mom might still offer her unsolicited opinions on your weight and wardrobe, and Dad might still only start a conversation if it has to do with your car. The key is to love the best parts of them and learn to accept the rest. Here are 14 **Stealth** Healthy ways to forge an adult relationship with your parents and enhance what might not always have been the strongest of bonds.

5 1) Think of them as fellow adults, rather than as your parents. If your parents still treat you like a kid, despite the fact that you have kids of your own, you may have to help them let you "grow up." "Feeling and acting like an adult around your parents is the **cornerstone** of having an adult relationship with them," says Tina B. Tessina, Ph.D., a licensed psychotherapist in Long Beach, California, and author of *It Ends With You: Grow Up and Out of Dysfunction and The 10 Smartest Decisions a Woman Can Make Before 40*. "If you treat them as fellow adults, they're more likely to treat you like one." A simple way to do this is to ask yourself a question before each interaction with them: "How would I act in this situation if Mom or Dad was a friend or an acquaintance?" Then behave accordingly.

6 2) Talk to your parents as friends. If your parents still treat you like you're 6 or 16, it may feel funny to give up your role as the child. A good start is to model your conversations with

Mom and Dad on those you have with friends, says Dr. Tessina. "Don't limit your conversations strictly to family memories, or gossip about family members, or your personal life," she

> **crotchety** *adj.* easily annoyed or made slightly angry, grumpy 容易恼怒的
> **batty** *adj.* mad, eccentric 疯狂的，古怪的
> **seethe** *v.* to be violently excited or agitated 大为光火

advises. There's a whole wide world out there—why not explore it with Mom and Dad as you would with a friend? Current events, sports, work, local neighborhood issues, or national politics (if you happen to share the same views) are all fair game.

7 3) Keep your sense of humor. When you're dealing with your parents, laughter can be a lifesaver—both to help you handle the stress of dealing with sometimes **crotchety** individuals and to help you bond together. Tell a few jokes you know they'll enjoy, share some comics from the paper or e-mail with them, watch the Letterman show together. If you can laugh together, you're doing okay.

8 4) Tell your parents what bothers you. If you love your mom and dad but they drive you **batty**, your resentment can eat away at your relationship. So don't **seethe** silently. Communicate, with gentleness and respect. For instance, if your mom keeps calling you at work, tell her that your boss is starting to notice and, while you love talking to her during the day, it's beginning to affect your job performance. Arrange a call you can both count on at a mutually convenient time.

9 5) Don't ask your parents' advice or opinion unless you really want it. Sometimes, asking for a parent's advice is really a way of asking for Mom or Dad's approval. If that's the case, remember that you're an adult now, perfectly capable of choosing a living room carpet or a car on your own. If your parents are bent on offering you advice whether asked or not, smile, nod, and take it in (who knows—it may actually be helpful!). Focus on the fact that they have your best interest at heart. Then make your own choice—without guilt.

10 6) Don't ask your parents to help straighten out your latest personal or financial crisis. While you may depend on their emotional support, relying too much

upon their resources, rather than your own, can lead to mutual resentment, says Dr. Tessina. So get used to solving your problems, big or small, on your own. You'll be amazed how good doing it all by yourself can make you feel—and what a positive effect it can have on your relationship with your parents.

> **accomplishment** *n.* sth completed successfully 成就
> **hospice** *n.* a program of medical and emotional care for the terminally ill 收容所
> **volition** *n.* the capability of conscious choice and decision and intention 自决，自主

11   7) Create opportunities for exploring and uncovering memories. If your parents are older, look through old scrapbooks with them, asking them for stories about the people in the photos. "We help our parents discover the meaning in their lives by encouraging them to talk about their **accomplishments**, the high points in their lives, and the joys and sorrows they have experienced," says Tom Swanson, Ph.D., director of support services education at VistaCare, a **hospice** care provider in Scottsdale, Arizona.

12   8) Help your parents preserve their memories on video, audiocassette, or in a scrapbook. The finished product will not only be a testament to a renewed closeness between you, but also provides a wonderful legacy.

13   9) Express your appreciation for all your parents have done for you. Yes, Mom may be a buttinsky, but she always makes your favorite Christmas cookies. Dad is a bit of a stuffed shirt, but just the other day, he came to your rescue when your car died at the mall. The point is, your parents still do things for you that deserve your notice—and gratitude.

14   10) Rediscover and share mutual interests. When you were a kid, did you and your dad share a passion for a particular football team? Did you and your mother spend time each summer canning tomatoes? Make these happy memories the foundation for new, shared activities.

15   11) Be honest about who you are and what you want. Maybe there are things about your growing up that your parents regret. But as long as you don't regret it, they have to adjust. Be clear about who you want to be and help your parents accept you on your terms.

16   12) Look for common activities. Baking, shopping, hiking, skiing, carpentry, etc. At any age, sharing a common task or activity, and the stories it engenders, is a great way to build closeness.

17   13) Do not allow them to channel guilt at you. If your parents are the type to complain about you never calling, never visiting, forgetting an uncle's birthday, not sending enough pictures, or whatever irks them that day, don't take the bait and feel guilty—unless you honestly regret the oversight. In which case, apologize immediately and seek a way to make amends. Otherwise, let it roll off your back. You have no obligation to play parent-child guilt games. You are a mature, independent adult, and act on your own **volition**.

14) Grant them their independence too. Sometimes it's the grown-up kid who doesn't want to cut the nurturing relationship off. If you are past 25 and still find it necessary to talk to Mom every night, or immediately turn to your dad for a house repair rather than your spouse, or automatically assume your parents will baby-sit the children whenever you need to be out, then you may be the problem, not your folks. They deserve freedom too.

(Words: 1286)

• Second Reading •

Directions: Read the text again more carefully to find enough information for Exercises I, II & III.

Exercise I True or False
Directions: Please state whether the following statements are true or not (T/F) according to the text.

1. It is easier to maintain good relationship between parents and adult children than between parents and teenagers.
2. When children grow up to be adults, their relationship with parents requires some change.
3. When your parents still treat you like a kid despite that you have your own kids, you should treat them as your kids in return.
4. When talking with parents, adult children should limit the conversations strictly to family affairs, never mentioning current evens or national policies.
5. As an adult child, you should never share your worries or upsets with your parents.
6. Though grown up, you should always ask your parents' advice or opinion, because they are more experienced than you.
7. When parents are old, adult children should encourage them to talk about their own accomplishments.
8. You should take every chance to express your gratitude to your parents.
9. When parents are complaining you rarely calling home, you should always feel guilty to them.
10. When you are over 25, you should tackle problems on your own instead of turning to your parents for help.

Exercise II Word Inference

Directions: Often you can guess the meaning of a word/expression by reading the words around it. Please read the given sentence to see how each word/expression in bold type is used in the text. Then choose the answer that is closest in meaning to the bold-faced word/expression.

1. Of course you love your parents—that's a **given**.

   A. certainty

   B. gift

   C. guarantee

   D. qualification

2. …You already have the basic **underpinnings**—love and shared memories.…

   A. conditions

   B. foundation

   C. construction

   D. elements

3. If your parents are **bent on offering** you advice whether asked or not, smile, nod, and take in.

   A. concentrated on offering

   B. determined to offer

   C. inclined to offer

   D. insisting on offering

4. The finished product will not only be a testament to a renewed closeness between you, but also provides a wonderful **legacy**.

   A. legal tender

   B. wealth

   C. property

   D. heritage

5. … or whatever irks them that day, don't take the bait and feel guilty—unless you honestly regret the **oversight**.

   A. mistake

   B. negligence

   C. fault

   D. guilt

6. Part of the evolution requires **forging** a new relationship, one…

   A. establishing

   B. smiting

   C. managing

   D. making up

7. … your **resentment** can eat away at your relationship.

   A. bitterness

   B. annoyance

   C. impatience

   D. indignation

8. But as long as you don't regret it, they have to **adjust**.

   A. forget the past

   B. make changes accordingly

   C. adapt themselves to the present reality

   D. forgive children's wrong deeds in the past

9. Do not allow them to **channel** guilt at you.

   A. relieve

   B. hide

   C. lead

   D. bring

10. Yes, Mom may be a **buttinsky**, but she always makes your favorite Christmas cookies.

    A. a person always busy with his own affairs

    B. a person always busy with other's unimportant things

    C. a person always busy with other's important things

    D. a person rarely busy with others' affairs

Exercise III Discussion

Directions: Please discuss the following questions in pairs or groups.

1. What do you think of the advice given by the writer? Do you agree with him / her?
2. Do you have problems with your parents? In what way do you want to solve the problems?

Text B

How to Mend a Broken Friendship: Reach Out to Old Friends

By Patricia Skalka

Warming-up Exercises

☞ How do you understand the proverb "A friend in need is a friend indeed"?
☞ What does "a fair weather friend" mean?

• First reading •

Directions: Now please read the following passage as fast as you can and summarize the main idea.

1   Growing up across the street from each other in Twin Falls, Idaho, Lisa Fry and Paula Turner never doubted their friendship would last forever. But after Fry married, moved to New York City and had a baby, her letters to Turner suddenly went unanswered. "Do you think I've somehow offended her?" Fry asked her husband.

2   Turner, meanwhile, had convinced herself she was no longer important to Fry. "She's got a family now," she told herself. "We're just too different to be close like before."

3   Finally, Fry summoned the courage to call her old friend. At first, the conversation was awkward, yet soon they both admitted that they missed each other. A month later, they got together and quickly fell into their old habit of laughing and sharing confidences.

4   "Thank goodness I finally took action," Fry says. "We both realized we were as important to each other as ever."

5   There are good reasons to cherish our friendships. Some years ago a public-opinion research firm, Roper Starch Worldwide, asked 2007 people to identify one or two things that said the most about themselves. __A__.

6   "A well-established friendship carries a long history of experience and interaction that defines who we are and keeps us connected," says Donald Pannen, executive officer of the Western Psychological Association. "It is a heritage we should protect."

7   Ironically, says Brant R. Burleson, professor of communication at Purdue University in

West Lafayette, Ind., "the better friends you are, the more likely you'll face conflicts." And the outcome can be precisely what you don't want—an end to the relationship.

<blockquote>
hygienist n. one who helps a dentist by cleaning patients' teeth and giving advice about keeping teeth healthy 保健专家
swallow your pride v. phr. to do sth even though it is embarrassing for you, because you have no choice 别顾面子了
relieved v. p.p. made easier to bear 松了口气
standstill n. a situation in which there is no movement or activity at all 停滞，僵持
reconciliation n. the reestablishing of cordial relations 和解
</blockquote>

8   The good news is that most troubled friendships can be mended. Here's what experts suggest:

9   __B__. It wasn't easy, but that's what Denise Moreland of Hickam Air Force Base in Hawaii did when a friendship turned sour. For nearly four months, Moreland, 45, had watched over Nora Huizenga's two young daughters, who were living with their father on the base, while Huizenga, 40, completed training as a dental **hygienist** in Nevada. "I felt honored to be asked to step in," Moreland says.

10   When Huizenga returned at Christmas, Moreland recalls, "I had so much to tell her, but she never called." One daughter had a birthday party, but Moreland wasn't invited. "I felt like I'd been used," she says.

11   At first, Moreland vowed to avoid Huizenga. Then she decided to **swallow her pride** and let her friend know how she felt. Huizenga admitted that she'd been so worried about being separated from her family that she'd been blind to what her friend had done to help her. Today she says, "I would never have figured out what happened if Denise hadn't called me on it."

12   When a friend hurts you, your instinct is to protect yourself. But that makes it harder to patch up problems, explains William Wilmot, author of Relational Communication. "Most of us are **relieved** when differences are brought out in the open."

13   Apologize when you're wrong—even if you've also been wronged. No one should allow himself to be emotionally abused by anyone. But over the course of a friendship, even the best people make mistakes. "A relationship can grind to a **standstill** if the offender refuses to make the first move at **reconciliation**," Wilmot explains. "Under these circumstances, it may be best if the wronged person takes the initiative and apologizes—for getting upset, for not understanding the friend's circumstances. __C__."

14   That's what happened to a 29-year-old salesman from Deerfield, Ill., when a dispute over unpaid rent threatened his friendship with a college pal. Because the salesman and two roommates all signed the lease, each was responsible for the debt. After graduation, the

salesman tried to **cajole** his friend into paying up. Finally, when the landlord threatened to sue for the **arrears**, the salesman called his friend, yelling, "This is no joke! You're ruining my credit."

> **cajole** *v.* gradually persuade sb to do sth by being nice to them, or making promises to them 哄劝某人做某事
> **arrears** *n.* money that you owe sb because you have not made regular payments at the correct time 逾期欠款
> **gerontology** *n.* the scientific study of old age and its effects on the body 老年病学
> **tolerance** *n.* the quality of accepting other people's rights to their own opinions, beliefs, or actions 宽容
> **slight** *v.* to offend someone by treating them rudely or without respect 轻视，忽略

15 Later he regretted his outburst. He knew his friend was not trying to hurt him—he was just being irresponsible. "Even though my friend should have apologized first for the aggravation he had caused me, I shouldn't have lost my temper. I didn't want this to destroy our friendship," he says. When the salesman called to apologize, the friend admitted he was wrong. He apologized and paid the debt.

16 Experts agree that one of the worst things you can do when you're upset is to start a fight. "We don't think clearly when we're arguing," says Michael Lang, a professional mediator in Pittsburgh. Instead, says Lang, ask: "What's going on? This doesn't make sense."

17 ___D___. Sociologist Rebecca Adams of the University of North Carolina at Greensboro and Rosemary Blieszner, professor of **gerontology** and family studies at the Virginia Polytechnic Institute and State University in Blacksburg, interviewed 53 adults who each had many friendships lasting decades. "We were curious how these people managed to sustain strong friendships for so long," says Blieszner.

18 **Tolerance** is the key, the researchers learned. The subjects also didn't let problems get blown out of proportion. "It's surprising how often a dispute results from a simple misunderstanding," adds psychotherapist Anne Frenkel.

19 Jan Yager, author of *Friendshifts: The Power of Friendship and How It Shapes Our Lives*, recalls what happened after her father died and a close friend didn't attend the funeral. "I felt hurt and disappointed," she says.

20 Later Yager learned that her friend hadn't come to the service because she was still distraught over her own father's death. "My perspective changed entirely," says Yager. "Rather than feeling **slighted**, I empathized with her."

21 Accept that friendships change. A few years ago, Cindy Lawson, 34, of Chicago, and a close friend decided to co-host a friend's bridal shower. The two women agreed to share the work and the cost. Then the friend, an attorney, took a new, more demanding job. Total responsibility for the shower fell to Lawson.

22 On the Saturday of the shower, Lawson did all the party decorating, then prepared dinner for 35 guests. Her co-host did not arrive from her office until shortly before the

event. __E__.

23   Lawson was furious. But deep down, she did not want to break off ties. The two women were in a book club together, had many common friends and enjoyed dinners out together with their husbands. Instead, Lawson decided to remain friends—but not close friends.

> **nurture** *v.* to help grow or develop; cultivate 培养
> **outrank** *v.* to take precedence or surpass others in rank 超过 (级别高于)
> **screw up** *v. phr.* to make a bad mistake or do something very stupid 搞砸了

24   "Friendships change as our needs and lifestyles change," Wilmot observes. "It's healthy to have a host of friends and to sometimes shift the status of one or another."

25   Making friends can sometimes seem easy, says Yager. The hard part is keeping the connections strong during the natural ups and downs that affect all relationships. Her suggestion: Consider friendship an honor and a gift, and worth the effort to treasure and **nurture**.

(Words: 1155)

• Second Reading •

Directions: Read the text again more carefully to find enough information for Exercises I, II, III, IV & V.

Exercise I Understanding Text Organization

Directions: You may find there are a few sentences (segments) missing from the passage. Read the article through and decide where the following sentences should go.

1. Later her friend complained about the cost
2. See things from your friend's point of view
3. Friends far **outranked** homes, jobs, clothes and cars
4. **Swallow your pride**
5. When you apologize, give your friend the opportunity to admit that he'd **screwed up**

Exercise II Multiple-Choice Questions

Directions: Please choose the best answer from the four choices given.

1. According to Roper Starch's research, _____ far outranked homes, jobs, clothing, etc.
   A. parents

B. friends

C. life

D. money

2. In Brant R. Burleson's opinion, the better friends you are, the more likely you will _____.

   A. understand each other

   B. enjoy the company of the other

   C. like to be together with the other

   D. have conflicts with each other

3. Experts agree that _____ is the worst thing you can do when you are depressed.

   A. to start a fight

   B. to blame your friend

   C. to turn to parents' help

   D. to burst out crying

4. According to the researchers, _____ is the key to maintain friendship.

   A. kindness

   B. tolerance

   C. respect

   D. consideration

5. Making friends is _____ than keeping the connections strong over the time.

   A. more difficult

   B. more enjoyable

   C. easier

   D. more demanding

Exercise III   Word Matching

Directions: Please choose from among the supplied words to explain the original forms of the boldfaced words in the following sentences.

A. mend   B. contract   C. legacy   D. secrets   E. disagreeable

1. A month later, they got together and quickly fell into their old habit of laughing and sharing **confidences**.

2. It is a **heritage** we should protect.

3. It wasn't easy, but that's what Denise Moreland of Hickam Air Force Base in Hawaii did when a friendship turned **sour**.

4. When a friend hurts you, your instinct is to protect yourself. But that makes it harder to **patch up** problems, explains William Wilmot, author of Relational Communication.
5. Because the salesman and two roommates all signed the **lease**, each was responsible for the debt

Exercise IV Short-Answer Questions

Directions: Please answer the following questions briefly in your own words.

1. According to the experts, the closer friends are, the more likely they will quarrel, then what should we do to keep alive our friendship?
2. Do you think it right to apologize first even if you are wronged by your friends?
3. What is the key to maintaining lasting friendship?

Exercise V Discussion

Directions: Please discuss the following question in pairs or groups.

Try to think of 5 to 10 ways to mend a broken friendship.

Text C

Is Your Marriage in Trouble?

By Edwin Kiester, Jr., and Sally Valente Kiester

1 One evening when Linda Bunfield of Evergreen, Colo., asked her husband about his workday, he shrugged, mumbling something about being exhausted. It was the second time in a few days that Dennis had kept to himself like that.

2 Linda knew something was bothering him, but he wouldn't talk about it. To her this was yet another warning sign that their marriage needed improvement.

3 The next day she signed them up for a weekend couples' workshop given by Howard Markman at the University of Denver. There Dennis admitted he had work problems but "didn't want to burden" Linda with them. The workshop convinced him that they needed to share such concerns in order to have a strong marriage.

4 "People think marriages end with an affair or something equally explosive," says John Gottman, author of *Why Marriages Succeed or Fail*. "In fact, most end gradually, sliding down a slope of complaint, criticism, defensiveness and withdrawal until it's difficult to scramble back up. Yet there are usually early warnings that the relationship could be headed for trouble."

"Apparently I have done something to upset you."

5 Here are some of the most common warning lights that can alert you to take stock of your marriage:

6 **Separate Date Books** Linda Bunfield acknowledges that she and Dennis had been keeping "his" and "her" calendars. Each had a full schedule that, however unintentionally, excluded the other. In these hectic times, going separate ways is commonplace. It can also be a warning of possible breakdown ahead, according to therapist Michele Weiner-Davis, author of *Divorce Busting*. "Careers, children, hobbies, volunteer work—people put all these things ahead of their relationships," Weiner-Davis says. Her suggestion: an "our" calendar that puts your relationship first. Make it a priority to pencil in dates for dinner out, day trips and just spending time together at home.

7 **Thinking the Worst** In the early days of a marriage, spouses assume only the finest of motives for the other's actions. Take, for instance, the new husband who's late arriving for dinner. He's probably stuck in traffic, his wife thinks, or he probably had to stay longer at work. When he arrives, no matter what time, she greets him warmly.

8 Later in the marriage, however, as dinners grow cold and the kids are hungry, she becomes annoyed. He could have called, she may think. He never considers anyone but himself. Or she broods about other, less kindly explanations—perhaps another woman or a stop at the neighborhood bar.

9 "It's a bad sign when partners don't give each other the benefit of the doubt," says Markman, co-author of *Fighting for Your Marriage*. In solid relationships partners cut each other some slack.

10 **No More Pinches** When Pat and Tom Sanders walk down the street, friends watch with amusement. The Palo Alto, Calif., couple have been married 33 years, yet they still walk hand in hand.

11   When a relationship is new, there's plenty of touching. The two can scarcely pass each other without an affectionate pat. But for many couples, that casual intimacy eventually vanishes. "They don't pinch each other anymore," Gottman says. "They don't giggle together over private jokes or offer compliments such as 'Thanks for that wonderful dinner last night.'"

12   **Growing Out of Touch**   One workshop exercise at the Seattle Marital and Family Institute has couples answer such questions as "Who's your partner's enemy at work?" and "What's your partner's favorite way to spend an evening?" One husband was stumped when asked, "What are your partner's concerns and worries?"

13   It's potential trouble when a spouse no longer knows a partner's likes and dislikes, or doesn't recognize issues that make the partner anxious.

14   **Gritted Teeth**   A Seattle woman's husband would frequently switch on the television after dinner. In the early days of their marriage, she protested regularly. "But after a while," she says, "I gritted my teeth and put up with it. But the anger never went away."

15   Says Markman: "Too much peace can lead to a cold, distant relationship. Unless the partners speak up and resolve their differences and fight for their marriage, eventually there'll be an explosion—or a walkout."

16   **History Turns Sardonic**   Alan met Lyllian when he came to pick up her roommate for a date. Marge and Tom met when he and his buddies gathered to get a look at the new teachers who'd come to their small Iowa town. Couples delight in telling these stories, often with laughter and affection.

17   But with other couples, sometimes the laughter disappears, and the whimsical tone gives way to sarcasm: "She trapped me—that's how it happened," or "He chased me until I got tired of running." This is a tip-off that shouldn't be ignored. In fact, some marriage researchers say they can predict which couples are headed for a breakup simply by asking questions such as "How did you happen to get married?" and then watching their reactions.

18   If a warning signal lights up on your marital dashboard, here's what the experts advise:

19   **Speak Softly**   Don't challenge your spouse. Introduce your concern gently and with politeness and respect.

20   One couple in a Gottman workshop had just had a second child. As the mother was nursing the newborn in bed, with the older child lying between his parents, the husband suddenly realized there were now two bodies separating him from his wife. Sensing something was wrong, she asked, "What's the problem, John?"

21   "Oh, I'm just having a pity party," he replied.

22   "That was a wonderful answer," Gottman says. "His wife understood he was feeling

neglected without his withdrawing or complaining."

23   **Don't Wait**   When you know things have gotten off track, speak up: "I don't like the way things have been going between us lately. Can we talk about it?" Couples who stay happily married only let a few difficult days pass before they look for a resolution.

24   **Do a "Blamectomy"**   "Remove blame from the discussion," Gottman advises. "Say, 'This is what's bothering me, what can we do about it?' Not, 'You lout! Why do you behave that way?'"

25   **Be Flexible**   Smart couples look for ways to ease tensions before they escalate out of control. In that regard, says Markman, "a little give makes a big difference."

(Words: 1024)

Exercise I Discussion

Directions: Please discuss the following questions in pairs or groups.

1. Do you agree with the writer's advices on how to save the endangered marriage? What is your opinion on this?
2. What role do you think husbands and wives play in the marriage?
3. The divorce rate is on the rise in China. How do you account for this phenomenon?

Exercise II Writing

Directions: The articles in this unit are about dealing with interpersonal relationships. Do you think the tips given are effective? Choose one topic and offer your ways of saving communication crisis by writing a composition in about 150 words.

UNIT SEVEN

CAMPUS LIFE IN THE USA

Target of the Unit

☞ To get a glimpse of American college life
☞ To practice reading skills
☞ To enlarge your vocabulary

1) LEAD IN

Directions: In this unit, you will read 3 passages about campus life in the USA. Read them and get a glimpse of American youths' college life.

2) DISCUSSION

What do you expect for your college life?

Text A

There's More to College Life Than Classes: Get Involved!

By Robin L. House

Warming-up Exercises

☞ Have you been actively involved in extracurricular activities on campus? Why/why not?

First reading

Directions: Now please read the following passage as fast as you can and summarize the main idea.

1   The life of an average college student is filled with writing papers, reading books, researching information, and attending classes. College would be pretty dull if this was it. In addition to the demands of classes, many students are sustaining relationships, preparing meals and housekeeping duties, dealing with family **obligations**, and other personal responsibilities. It can be both a fun and stressful period in a person's life. There is pressure to get good grades, cooperate with new people, and manage the many freedoms that accompany college life. And if this all wasn't enough, it changes from semester to semester. **Transitions** and changes come with the territory. A college student must be able to move outside their **comfort zone**.

> **obligation** *n.* promise, duty or condition indicating what action should be taken 义务，职责，责任
> **transition** *n.* change, from one condition to another 变化, 过渡
> **comfort zone** *n. phr.* One's comfort zone refers to the set of environments and behaviors with which one is comfortable, without creating a sense of risk. A person's personality can be described by his or her comfort zones. Highly successful persons may routinely step outside their comfort zones, to accomplish what they wish. A comfort zone is a type of mental conditioning that causes a person to create and operate mental boundaries that are not real. Such boundaries create an unfounded sense of security. Like inertia, a person who has established a comfort zone in a particular axis of his or her life, will tend to stay within that zone without stepping outside of it. To step outside a person's comfort zone, they must experiment with new and different behaviors, and then experience the new and different responses that then occur within his environment. [心理学]舒适区
> **extracurricular** *adj.* outside the regular course 课外的
> **academy** *n.* society of distinguished scholars 学会

2   I learned a long time ago the importance of being involved in **extracurricular** school activities. At first it was difficult for me because I was quiet and shy. I learned that if you are quiet you won't get anything you want or need. I worked on becoming more outgoing and assertive. My friends, playing soccer, and editing the school newspaper got me through high school. In college I had a paid job as the copy editor of the campus newspaper. I had internships with radio station KWMU and the National **Academy** of Television Arts and Sciences. No matter what you are doing right now, you need to take a look at what you could be doing on your college campus for yourself and the betterment of the institution.

3   There are many reasons to become involved on your college campus in any way that you

see best for you. It may be with a **fraternity** or **sorority**. Perhaps it might be athletics, student government, or an internship. What ever you choose it will give you good experiences, which you can use on your resume. It will also help you meet other people. And when the stress levels intensify, it will give you the support you need to hang in there until the end—graduation.

> **fraternity** *n.* a chiefly social organization of men students at a college or university, usually designated by Greek letters 男大学生组织，男生会
> **sorority** *n.* a chiefly social organization of women students at a college or university, usually designated by Greek letters 女大学生组织，女生会
> **Braille** *n.* The braille system is a method that is widely used by blind people to read and write. Braille was devised in 1821 by Louis Braille, a Frenchman 盲文

4   How to find what is right for you? First, what are your interests and strengths? What field of study are you interested in pursuing? Then, talk to other students in your classes, dorm or in the library. Check with college professors for opportunities. Check out the campus newspaper. The possibilities are almost endless. If you look you will find something that is right for you. (Disclaimer: Try not to overextend yourself. Balance is the key here.)

5   Working for the Federation cause with other blind students is another way to get involved. For example, in St. Louis at the University of Missouri St. Louis, a group of us were members of the Missouri Association of Blind Students. One of our members wanted to get the Coke machines labeled in **Braille**. He could not make any progress with the University administration. We devised a plan to make the labels ourselves. The University agreed and bought the supplies, breakfast, and lunch. A group of six of us labeled over 700 labels. Now all the machines on both campuses are labeled in Braille.

6 Then we held a scholarship seminar where we invited other students and distributed NFB of Missouri and NFB National scholarship applications in November. During Disability Awareness Week we **put together** a display on Blindness. There was a simulation of finding information using a cassette recorder. The Society of the Blind brought **goggles** which simulated different eye conditions. We distributed cards with the Braille alphabet. We worked together to give students the right to select and train readers of their choosing. We are not finished. There is more work to do on our campus. Our goal is to make it better for current and future blind students.

> **put together** *v. phr.* to construct; create 搞出来（一个活动等）
> **goggles** *n. pl.* Goggles or safety glasses are forms of protective eyewear that usually enclose or protect the eye area in order to prevent particulates, water or chemicals 护目镜

7 It is important for students to become active participants on their college campuses. Whether you pledge a fraternity or sorority, find an internship, get a job or begin working with other blind students, you will help your campus to be a better place. Keep those grades up and learn as much as you can. A higher education is an avenue for you to achieve your goals and dreams. As you can see, there's more to college life than classes. Get involved!

(Words: 702)

Second Reading

Directions: Read the text again more carefully to find enough information for Exercises I, II & III.

Exercise I   True or False

Directions: Please state whether the following statements are true or false (T/F) according to what you've found in the text.

1. The life of an average college student is focused on study.
2. College life is boring and stressful in the author's eyes.
3. Quiet students could never get what they want or need at college.
4. The author was a quiet and shy student when she was in college.
5. Being involved in extracurricular activities will give students good experiences.

6. As long as they want, the students can always find something that's suitable for them on campus.
7. But getting involved on campus will definitely intensify the stress levels.
8. Helping the others who are in need is also a good way to get involved.
9. The author seems to be a blind person.
10. Getting involved will overextend the students and affect their study.

Exercise II Word Inference

Directions: Often you can guess the meaning of a word/expression by reading the words around it. Please read the given sentence to see how each word/expression in bold type is used in the text. Then choose the answer that is closest in meaning to the bold-faced word/expression.

1. In addition to the demands of classes, many students are **sustaining** relationships, preparing meals and housekeeping duties, dealing with family obligations, and other personal responsibilities.

    A. supporting

    B. suffering

    C. surviving

    D. maintaining

2. There is pressure to get good grades, cooperate with new people, and **manage** the many freedoms that accompany college life.

    A. control

    B. make use of

    C. deal with

    D. succeed in getting

3. Transitions and changes come with the **territory**.

    A. land owned by a particular country

    B. area claimed or dominated by a person or an animal

    C. area of knowledge or activity

    D. a particular situation, place, etc.

4. I worked on becoming more outgoing and **assertive**.

    A. aggressive

    B. strong and confident

C. easygoing

D. eloquent

5. I had **internships** with radio station KWMU and the National Academy of Television Arts and Sciences.

   A. short-time jobs done to gain experience

   B. close relationships

   C. contracts

   D. interviews

6. And when the stress levels **intensify**, it will give you the support you need to hang in there until the end—graduation.

   A. reduce

   B. continue

   C. maintain

   D. increase in degree or strength

7. **Disclaimer:** Try not to overextend yourself. Balance is the key here.

   A. a statement that says one is not responsible for sth

   B. a statement that says one is not involved in sth

   C. a statement that says one does not know about sth

   D. a statement that aims to give some advice or warning

8. The Society of the Blind brought goggles which **simulated** different eye conditions.

   A. compared

   B. improved

   C. copied

   D. produced

9. Whether you **pledge** a fraternity or sorority, find an internship, get a job or begin working with other blind students, you will help your campus to be a better place.

   A. join

   B. plead

   C. pray

   D. vow

10. A higher education is an **avenue** for you to achieve your goals and dreams.

    A. street

    B. path

    C. revenue

    D. beginning

Exercise III   Discussion

Directions: Please discuss the following questions in pairs or groups.

1. Do you agree with the author that students should get more involved in extracurricular activities than just being occupied by study? Why/why not?
2. Do you think it is possible to strike a balance between study and extracurricular activities? If yes, how?

Text B

College Survival Tips for the Nontraditional College Students' Successful Entry to College Life and a College Education

By Unnamed Author

Warming-up Exercises

☞ What kind of college survival tips you had got before you entered the college?
☞ And what tips will you give to those who are about to go to college?

• First reading •

Directions: Now please read the following passage as fast as you can and summarize the main idea.

1   __A__ . However, a growing trend in the nontraditional student population would indicate a large number of older students are taking advantage of opportunities once thought to be available **primarily** to the fresh out of High School. Nontraditional students (any student over the age of 25) are **flocking** to many of the nation's

> **primarily** *adv.* mainly 主要地
> **flock** *n.* gather, move together in great numbers 成群结队

institutions of higher learning to avail themselves of the benefits of a college education. However, the life of a nontraditional student is usually quite different from one fresh out of High School. Oftentimes, college life is a bit more difficult to balance for the older student, **juggling** school classes, college requirements, and final exams with the sometimes more complex issues of life itself.

> **juggle** *v.* to keep (more than two activities, for example) in motion or progress at one time 许多事情都兼顾
> **hold true** *v. phr.* (*colloq*) be true 是真实的
> **acquaint oneself with** *v. phr.* get familiar with 搞熟关系
> **feat** *n.* a specialized skill; a knack 本事

2   But, the life of a nontraditional can be every bit as rewarding, if the return to college is thoughtfully and carefully planned. Some thoughts **hold true** for all students, no matter at what age. Other suggestions apply more to the older student.

3   For the most positive college experience, a nontraditional student would do well to consider the following guidelines:

4   1) Plan ahead—phone or write for a college catalog, a list of courses offered, a college handbook, and any other literature the school's admissions office has to offer. Read up on as much as possible, to **acquaint** yourself with what lies ahead.

5   2) Look for departments or organizations designed specifically for older students. A college or university might have special clubs, or you might find help through some type of student support services.

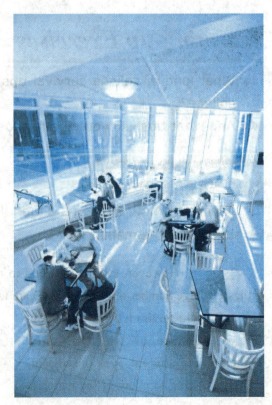

6   3) __B__. Plan to personally meet and visit with your financial aid counselor, admissions personnel, and anyone connected with some of the departments and organizations you've got your eye on. It is especially helpful to visit with professors within the department you think you will major.

7   4) If you're moving to a new town for school, try to move in a few weeks before registration. Allow yourself plenty of time to unpack and get settled in. Moving is quite a significant **feat**, all by itself. You might also want to get to know your new neighbors, as well. __C__.

8   5) Walk around campus and acquaint yourself better with the layout of the campus and with places you know you'll need to visit later. Take time to start meeting a few people, so you'll start feeling more settled and comfortable in your new surroundings.

> **frustrating** *adj.* preventing realization or attainment of a desire 令人沮丧的
> **stroll** *n.* slow leisurely walk 散步，闲逛
> **by all means** *phr.* (*fml*) yes, of course, certainly 一定

9   6) Registration Day—don't sweat it. Registration day is almost always long, boring and **frustrating**! It won't be just because you're not the "traditional" student, either. It's always chaos for almost everyone involved. After registration is complete, get your books and start familiarizing yourself with what's to come. Then, **stroll** around campus again, and try to locate where your classes will be held.

10   7) Don't be afraid to meet and get to know other students—even the "youngsters." Walk the campus, spend some time in the Student Center, and get to know your new neighbors, as well.

11   8) Take time to meet all of your teachers and start getting to know them during the first couple of weeks of classes. Get a feel for who they are and what they expect from their students and their classes. Let them get to know you, too, as an individual. Many teachers have a high respect for older students, and this will be in your favor. And, **by all means**, keep in touch with teachers throughout the term. If you have problems, like a personal illness or illness in the family, let your instructors know as soon as possible. This helps you stay on top of your education, instead of getting buried under it.

12   9) __D__. Most teachers will hand out a course syllabus (schedule and requirements) at the beginning of the term, so students will know what to expect. Make notes of special assignments, exams and special projects and when they become due. Try to start these special projects and assignments early. Although every student will sometimes have problems finishing an assignment or making it to an exam, older students with additional responsibilities of family and work may find themselves more likely to hit a bump in the road than younger students. Again, keep in touch with your instructors! This could mean the difference in having extra time to complete an assignment or exam, or having to take a failing grade for something missed due to circumstances beyond your control.

13   10) Finally, allow yourself room to be human—to be yourself! Don't try to be something you're not. Many older students try too hard to fit in, joining social clubs and hanging out with the younger students all of the time. You don't have to do this, unless it's just something you really want to do. If you want to do it, that's fine. But you don't have to pretend to be "one of the kids." You have a lot to offer, by just being yourself.

Many students will look up to you, admiring your initiative and zeal for working for your education. __E__.

> **keep sth in perspective** *v. phr.* to keep sth in a way that doesn't exaggerate any aspect 正确看待问题

14 Above everything else, just be yourself. Think of college as simply one aspect of your life, rather than making it your entire life. This will help you **keep everything in perspective**.

15 Prepare before you go, yes, then just do your best and enjoy a very meaningful time of your life.

(Words: 962)

· Second Reading ·

Directions: Read the text again more carefully to find enough information for Exercises I, II, III, IV & V.

Exercise I Understanding Text Organization

Directions: You may find there are a few sentences (segments) missing from the passage. Read the article through and decide where the following sentences should go.

1. Make a visit to campus before you enroll.
2. Many others will simply look past you, because you don't "fit in."
3. Some of them will probably be seasoned back-to-college folks, who can offer you advice and support.
4. In a world where youth rules, a stroll down many college and university campuses would seem to confirm the fact that youth, in fact, do have strength in numbers.
5. Give yourself plenty of time to complete assignments.

Exercise II Multiple-Choice Questions

Directions: Complete each of the following statements with the best choice given.

1. College life is more difficult for nontraditional students mainly because they _____.
   A. have more classes to attend
   B. have to meet higher college requirements

  C. are not as energetic as the younger students

  D. have additional responsibilities of family and work

2. Before you get registered, you should try to _____.

  A. acquaint yourself with all your teachers

  B. make a visit to campus

  C. meet and get to know other students

  D. call the admissions personnel

3. If you keep in touch with your instructors, in circumstances beyond your control _____.

  A. you may get extra time to complete an assignment or exam

  B. you may not miss any requirements

  C. you may get timely help from the teachers

  D. you may still have to take a failing grade for something missed

4. The best way to fit in for the older students is to _____.

  A. join as many social clubs as possible

  B. hang out as often as possible with the younger ones

  C. be themselves and show their strengths

  D. get on good terms with their instructors

5. It seems that the most important suggestion given in the text is _____.

  A. to be yourself

  B. to plan ahead

  C. to keep in touch with instructors

  D. to mix with younger students

Exercise III Word Matching

Directions: Please choose from among the supplied words to explain the original forms of the boldfaced words in the following sentences.

  A. take out luggage B. make use of C. pamphlet D. respect E. advisor

1. Nontraditional students (any student over the age of 25) are flocking to many of the nation's institutions of higher learning to **avail themselves of** the benefits of a college education.

2. Plan ahead—phone or write for a college catalog, a list of courses offered, a college handbook, and any other **literature** the school's admissions office has to offer.

3. Plan to personally meet and visit with your financial aid **counselor**, admissions

personnel, and anyone connected with some of the departments and organizations you've got your eye on.

4. Allow yourself plenty of time to **unpack** and get settled in.
5. Many students will **look up to** you, admiring your initiative and zeal for working for your education.

Exercise IV   Short-Answer Questions

Directions: Please answer the following questions briefly in your own words.

1. Who are the so-called nontraditional students?
2. "This helps you stay on top of your education, instead of getting buried under it." What does the sentence mean?
3. What does the expression "to hit a bump on the road" [12-(9)] mean?

Exercise V   Discussion

Directions: Please discuss the following questions in pairs or groups.

1. What tips given in the text may apply to you? Why?
2. Will you consider going back to study in college after you have graduated and worked for some years? Please give your reasons.

Text C

Commencement Address at Wellesley College

By Barbara Pierce Bush

1   Thank you very, very much, President Keohane. Mrs. Gorbachev, Trustees, faculty, parents, and I should say, Julia Porter, class president, and certainly my new best friend, Christine Bicknell—and, of course, the Class of 1990. I am really thrilled to be here today, and very excited, as I know all of you must be, that Mrs. Gorbachev could join us.

2   These—These are exciting times. They're exciting in Washington, and I have really looked forward to coming to Wellesley. I thought it was going to be fun. I never dreamt it

would be this much fun. So, thank you for that.

3   More than ten years ago, when I was invited here to talk about our experiences in the People's Republic of China, I was struck by both the natural beauty of your campus and the spirit of this place.

4   Wellesley, you see, is not just a place but an idea—an experiment in

excellence in which diversity is not just tolerated, but is embraced. The essence of this spirit was captured in a moving speech about tolerance given last year by a student body president of one of your sister colleges. She related the story by Robert Fulghum about a young pastor, finding himself in charge of some very energetic children, hits upon the game called "Giants, Wizards, and Dwarfs." "You have to decide now," the pastor instructed the children, "which you are—a giant, a wizard, or a dwarf?" At that, a small girl tugging at his pants leg, asked, "But where do the mermaids stand?" And the pastor tells her there are no mermaids. And she says, "Oh yes there are—they are. I am a mermaid."

5   Now this little girl knew what she was, and she was not about to give up on either her identity, or the game. She intended to take her place wherever mermaids fit into the scheme of things. "Where do the mermaids stand? All of those who are different, those who do not fit the boxes and the pigeonholes?" "Answer that question," wrote Fulghum, "And you can build a school, a nation, or a whole world." As that very wise young woman said, "Diversity, like anything worth having, requires effort—effort to learn about and respect difference, to be compassionate with one another, to cherish our own identity, and to accept unconditionally the same in others.

6   You should all be very proud that this is the Wellesley spirit. Now I know your first choice today was Alice Walker—guess how I know!—known for The Color Purple. Instead you got me—known for the color of my hair. Alice Walker's book has a special resonance here. At Wellesley, each class is known by a special color. For four years the Class of '90 has worn the color purple. Today you meet on Severance Green to say goodbye to all of that, to begin a new and a very personal journey, to search for your own true colors.

7   In the world that awaits you, beyond the shores of Waban—Lake Waban, no one can say what your true colors will be. But this I do know: You have a first class education from a first class school. And so you need not, probably cannot, live a "paint-by-numbers" life. Decisions

are not irrevocable. Choices do come back. And as you set off from Wellesley, I hope that many of you will consider making three very special choices.

8   The first is to believe in something larger than yourself, to get involved in some of the big ideas of our time. I chose literacy because I honestly believe that if more people could read, write, and comprehend, we would be that much closer to solving so many of the problems that plague our nation and our society.

9   And early on I made another choice, which I hope you'll make as well. Whether you are talking about education, career, or service, you're talking about life—and life really must have joy. It's supposed to be fun.

10 One of the reasons I made the most important decision of my life, to marry George Bush, is because he made me laugh. It's true, sometimes we've laughed through our tears, but that shared laughter has been one of our strongest bonds. Find the joy in life, because as Ferris Bueller said on his day off, "Life moves pretty fast; and ya don't stop and look around once in a while, ya gonna miss it."

11 (I'm not going to tell George ya clapped more for Ferris than ya clapped for George.)

12 The third choice that must not be missed is to cherish your human connections: your relationships with family and friends. For several years, you've had impressed upon you the importance to your career of dedication and hard work. And, of course, that's true. But as important as your obligations as a doctor, a lawyer, a business leader will be, you are a human being first. And those human connections—with spouses, with children, with friends—are the most important investments you will ever make.

13 At the end of your life, you will never regret not having passed one more test, winning one more verdict, or not closing one more deal. You will regret time not spent with a husband, a child, a friend, or a parent.

14 We are in a transitional period right now—We are in a transitional period right now, fascinating and exhilarating times, learning to adjust to changes and the choices we, men and women, are facing. As an example, I remember what a friend said, on hearing her husband complain to his buddies that he had to babysit. Quickly setting him straight, my friend told her husband that when it's your own kids, it's *not* called babysitting.

15 Now maybe we should adjust faster; maybe we should adjust slower. But whatever the era twenty—whatever the era, whatever the times, one thing will never change: fathers and mothers, if you have children, they must come first. You must read to your children, and you must hug your children, and you must love your children. Your success as a family, our success as a society, depends not on what happens in the White House, but on what happens inside your house.

16 For over fifty years, it was said that the winner of Wellesley's annual hoop race would be the first to get married. Now they say, the winner will be the first to become a C.E.O. Both—Both of those stereotypes show too little tolerance for those who want to know where the mermaids stand. So—So I want to offer a new legend: the winner of the hoop race will be the first to realize her dream—not society's dreams—her own personal dream.

17 And who—Who knows? Somewhere out in this audience may even be someone who will one day follow in my footsteps, and preside over the White House as the President's spouse—and I wish him well.

18 Well, the controversy ends here. But our conversation is only beginning. And a worthwhile conversation it has been. So as you leave Wellesley today, take with you deep thanks for the courtesy and the honor you have shared with Mrs. Gorbachev and with me.

19 Thank you. God bless you. And may your future be worthy of your dreams.

(Words: 1241)

Exercise I Discussion

Directions: Please discuss the following questions in pairs or groups.

1. What is the Wellesley spirit? How do you think about it?
2. What are the three choices Mrs. Bush hopes the graduating students will consider making? Will you make the same choices?
3. Though advocating more tolerance for diverse personal dreams, Mrs. Bush seems to lay more emphasis on the importance of traditional family values in this transitional period. Do you agree with her?

Exercise II Writing

Directions: Write a composition in about 150 words, making a comparison between your campus life and that in the USA.

UNIT EIGHT

LAW IN EVERYDAY LIFE

Target of the Unit

☞ To get a glimpse of the US legal system
☞ To practice reading skills
☞ To enlarge your vocabulary

1) LEAD IN

Directions: In this unit, you will read 3 passages about various aspects of US legal system in everyday life. Note how the American people react in a situation where law is resorted to for legal help.

2) DISCUSSION

What do you know about American legislature?

Text A

You're Being Duped

By Michael Crowley

Warming-up Exercises

☞ What is the function of taxation for a country?
☞ How should taxpayers' money be spent?

• First reading •

Directions: Now please read the following passage as fast as you can and summarize the main idea.

1   Imagine a law that gave members of Congress the power to **snoop** through your tax returns. Or worse, imagine if it let Congressional leaders designate anyone they wanted to go **peek** at your file down at IRS headquarters and learn all about your income, your family...your life.

> **dupe** v. to trick or deceive someone 欺骗, 愚弄
> **snoop** v. to try to find out about someone's private affairs by secretly looking in their house, examining their possessions etc 探听, 打探
> **peek** n. peep, a secret look 偷窥
> **nuts** adj. crazy 发狂的
> **provision** n. a condition in an agreement or law（法律）规定

2   Sound **nuts**? Well, just such a law was passed last November, allowing the heads of two Congressional committees to appoint "agents" of their choice (presumably staffers) to enter any IRS facility and look through the returns on file. And here's the excuse our legislators give: They didn't have a clue what they were voting on. "I did not know it was in the bill," Tom DeLay, the House Majority Leader, told his local newspaper. "I have no earthly idea how it got there," Senate Majority Leader Bill Frist said on a CBS news program. The really sad thing is, they're telling the truth.

3   Laws affecting your life are passed all the time by members of Congress who may not know just what is in the legislation. "We don't have a chance to read—let alone understand—some of the bills we're called upon to vote on," says Rep. Henry Waxman of California.

4   That's the story behind the IRS bill. It turns out that a House Appropriations Committee staffer added the one-sentence **provision** into a 2,000-page budget bill before Congress voted on it. Only after it was too late to change the legislation did someone in the office of North Dakota Sen. Kent Conrad read the fine print and notice the threat to privacy.

5   In this case, an immediate uproar embarrassed Congress into quickly repealing the provision. But plenty of bills become law virtually unnoticed. How many legislators realized that their vote almost two years ago on a

mammoth budget bill would cause a controversial change in gun-control law? Tucked into that legislation was a requirement that the records from background checks of gun buyers be destroyed within 24 hours, instead of 90 days. You can bet the gun lobby wasn't among those left in the dark.

> **mammoth** *adj.* extremely large 巨大的
> **obscene** *adj.* extremely unfair, immoral, or unpleasant, especially in a way that makes you angry 猥亵的
> **fiasco** *n.* an event that is completely unsuccessful, in a way that is very embarrassing or disappointing 惨败
> **arcane** *adj.* secret and known or understood by only a few people 神秘的，不可思议的

6 The fact is, there's no way that members of Congress or their legislative aides can comb through a massive bill in less than a couple of days. Yet they commonly get much less time to scrutinize bills that may, according to one veteran Congressional staffer, "get thrown together so quickly that there are handwritten crossouts or additions." Is this any way to run the government? "It's become **obscene**," says Arizona Sen. John McCain. It's also not an accident. In recent years, McCain says, Congressional leaders have made it harder to shine a light on what's in large, complicated bills. "We used to be able to demand that the bill be read [aloud]," says McCain. "And they changed the rules so you can't do that anymore."

7 To plenty of politicians, it's worth embarrassments like the IRS **fiasco** to keep their actions under wraps. That same bill with the tax-snooping provision was also loaded with pork, like $1.5 million for a project to determine the feasibility of transporting chilled water from Lake Ontario to two New York counties, and $70,000 for the Paper Industry International Hall of Fame in Appleton, Wisconsin. Rush the legislation through and there's less chance you'll get raised eyebrows.

8 But that's not the only trick being played. At times, the wording of bills is intended to cloud their real meaning. "Some of the language is so **arcane** that it takes a true expert [to understand]," McCain says.

9 Consider one section of a recent tax bill which purports to define a family member: "For purposes of this paragraph, an individual shall not be considered a common ancestor if...the individual is more than six generations removed from the youngest generation of shareholders who would (but for this clause) be members of the family." What does that actually mean? According to a tax specialist on Capitol Hill, it's probably language designed to give somebody a big new tax break.

10 The real heart of the problem, say Congressional watchdogs, is that the legislative process has become more opaque. There's less open debate, and there's more bill-writing by very small groups. "Leaders, their staffers, and in many cases the special interest lobbyists, will sit down and slap a bill together," says Norman Ornstein, a scholar at the American Enterprise

Institute. "They don't even concern themselves with whether it's bad or embarrassing because they won't be tested on it."

11   Usually the **shenanigans** go unnoticed. But a few years ago, Alaska Sen. Ted Stevens stuck a provision into a defense bill to allow the Air Force to lease fuel-tanker jets from Boeing. Several government studies suggested the deal would cost billions more than just buying the planes outright. But Boeing and a few Air Force officials lobbied hard for the lease arrangement, and the plan passed.

> **shenanigan** *n.* bad behaviour that is not very serious, or slightly dishonest activities 恶作剧，诡计
> **cushy** *adj.* a cushy job or life is very easy and does not need much effort 容易而赚钱的（工作）

12   That tanker deal wound up at the center of a huge scandal when it turned out that a key Pentagon official involved in the contract had been lining up **cushy** jobs at Boeing for relatives and for herself. She's now doing time in a federal prison. Maybe a little more open debate would have exposed the corruption before it got as far as it did. More time to examine bills is just the reform that Norman Ornstein wants to see. "Allowing a few people to tinker with bills at the eleventh hour is a recipe for crummy legislation," he says. "We should have a three-day waiting period before completed bills are voted on."

13   Good idea. But the best chance of reform starts with you. If you're bothered by this last-minute lawmaking, contact your legislators on Capitol Hill (all are listed at vote-smart.org). And remind them that how they vote will determine how you vote.

(Words: 960)

• Second Reading •

Directions: Read the text again more carefully to find enough information for Exercises I, II & III.

Exercise I True or False

Directions: Please state whether the following statements are true or not (T/F) according to the text.

1. Laws influencing people's life are passed all the time by members of the Congress who may not even know what is in the legislation.
2. Every law or legal document is passed before being thoroughly examined and scrutinized.

3. In fact, there are enough time for the members of Congress to examine the bills before they are passed.

4. When bills are voted, they will be read aloud to let every congressman know it clearly.

5. Sometimes, there are so many terminologies in the bills that only experts can understand the real meaning of them.

6. The real part of the problem is that the legislative process is too complicated and time-consuming.

7. To make bills objective, there should be more open debates, and more unprejudiced people involved in the bill-writing process.

8. Although government studies showed the tanker deal would be a great cost, Boeing and a few Air Force officials finally made the plan passed.

9. According to Norman Ornstein, less time should be given to the examination of the bills before they are voted on.

10. The Boeing tanker deal turned out to be a huge scandal.

Exercise II Word Inference

Directions: Often you can guess the meaning of a word/expression by reading the words around it. Please read the given sentence to see how each word/expression in bold type is used in the text. Then choose the answer that is closest in meaning to the bold-faced word/expression.

1. But plenty of bills become law **virtually** unnoticed.
   A. actually
   B. completely
   C. nobly
   D. vertically

2. Yet they commonly get much less time to **scrutinize** bill that may…
   A. observe
   B. discuss
   C. study
   D. inspect

3. At times, the wording of bills is intended to **cloud** their real meaning.
   A. hide
   B. clear

C. obscure

   D. cover with cloud

4. The real problem…is that the legislative process has become more **opaque**.

   A. difficult
   B. prejudiced
   C. complicated
   D. obscure

5. …to determine the **feasibility** of transporting chilled water…

   A. possibility
   B. certainty
   C. ability
   D. capacity

6. …according to one **veteran** Congressional staffer, "get thrown together so quickly that …

   A. aged
   B. experienced
   C. old
   D. retired

7. The real **heart** of the problem, say Congressional watchdogs, is...

   A. crux
   B. center
   C. focus
   D. essence

8. That tanker deal wound up at the center of a huge **scandal** when it turned out…

   A. misfortune

   B. error

   C. disgrace

   D. mistake

9. "Allowing a few people to **tinker with** bills at the eleventh hour is a recipe for crummy legislation."

   A. fix
   B. discuss with
   C. correct
   D. patch up

10. "Allowing a few people to tinker with bills at the eleventh hour is a recipe for **crummy** legislation."

    A. shabby
    B. nasty
    C. ordinary
    D. perfect

Exercise III Discussion

Directions: Please discuss the following questions in pairs or groups.

1. Who do you think decides the passage of bills?
2. What do you think of the legislative system in America?

Text B

Get' Em Off the Road!

By Michael Crowley

Warming-up Exercises

☞ What do you know about DUI?

• **First reading** •

Directions: Now please read the following passage as fast as you can and summarize the main idea.

1   When 19-year-old Sonja DeVries was killed waiting at a red light in Denver last summer, the young woman might have been thinking about her plans to become a child therapist. We'll never know. ___A___. The impact left Sonja brain dead. Her parents watched their only child die at the hospital. The driver of the truck, 55-year-old Ramon Romero, **stumbled** away from the crash: He was drunk, say prosecutors. Romero reportedly tested at more than double the state's legal blood-alcohol limit. He has **pleaded** not guilty and is scheduled for trial in February.

> **stumble** *v.* to miss one's step in walking or running; trip and almost fall; to proceed unsteadily or falteringly; flounder 踉跄
> **plead** *v.* to appeal earnestly; to declare oneself to be (guilty or not guilty) in answer to a charge 表示服罪或不服罪
> **kid-glove** *adj.* a way of treating someone kindly and carefully because they easily become upset 和蔼而小心的

2   ___B___. It turned out that Romero had been arrested for drunk driving a whopping six times before. Yet apparently this ticking time bomb had only been thrown in jail once, for a mere fifteen days. In fact, on the day he collided with Sonja DeVries, Romero had a perfectly valid driver's license.

3   How could that be? It turns out that lenient judges and **kid-glove** laws allowed Romero to slip through the cracks. According to Westword, a weekly newspaper in Denver, Romero's license was suspended several times, but by state law it was automatically handed back to him after a year. And following a couple of his arrests, judges let him plead to a lesser charge and accept alcohol counseling instead of jail time.

4   Most infuriating of all, Romero's story is far from unusual. Each year, it is estimated that

about 500,000 drunk-driver arrests in this country involve repeat offenders like him. In Minnesota alone in 2000, according to the *St. Paul Pioneer Press*, more than 1,000 drivers were arrested on alcohol-related charges for at least the sixth time. For 182 of those people it was at least their tenth **bust!**

> **bust** *n.* a situation in which the police go into a place in order to catch people doing something illegal 搜捕
> **misdemeanor** *n.* a crime—less serious than a felony—which is punishable by fine or imprisonment in a city or county jail rather than in a penitentiary 轻罪
> **felony** *n.* a serious crime such as murder 重罪
> **dig up** *v. phr* to find hidden or forgotten information by careful searching 挖掘信息
> **probation** *n.* a system that allows some criminals not to go to prison or to leave prison, if they behave well and see a probation officer regularly, for a particular period of time 缓刑

5 _____C_____. In 2001, drunk drivers killed over 5,000 innocent people—almost double the toll of the 9/11 terror attacks that year. At the same time, according to an estimate by the National Highway Traffic Safety Administration, drunk drivers cost our economy tens of billions of dollars, including higher expenses for medical care and such public services as police, fire and ambulance. The family budget even takes a direct hit, since drunk drivers boost almost everyone's auto insurance premium.

6 It's become a national disgrace for several reasons, but lax laws are among the biggest. In most states, a first offense is a **misdemeanor** that rarely leads to jail time. In a number of them, it takes three or more convictions before drunk driving becomes a **felony**. And even when you have repeat offenders who could get significant prison time, they're seldom handed the maximum sentence. In fact, in 2002, less than one percent of drunk drivers convicted in Massachusetts got two or more years in prison. Only 15 percent got any time at all. (Massachusetts has since changed its laws somewhat.)

7 Sometimes it's sloppy work by prosecutors that lets drunk drivers off easy. The *Albuquerque Journal* recently uncovered the case of a local man, Edward Sena, who pled to a first-offense DUI charge—despite the fact that it was his fifth drunk-driving conviction. It seems prosecutors failed to **dig up** the records that would have revealed all this. For this "first-time" offense, Sena never spent a day in jail or paid a penny in fines.

8 One of the quickest ways to reduce the work burden is to let defendants plead to lesser charges and receive **probation**. And that leads to

other problems.

> **overly** *adj.* to an excessive degree 过于
> **inebriated** *adj.* drunk 醉酒
> **enraged** *adj.* very angry 恼火的

9   An investigation by *The Washington Post* showed how easily drunk drivers in nearby Montgomery County, Maryland, can game the system. More often than not, the judge sentenced the offenders to probation if they agreed to undergo some sort of treatment. __D__. Yep, essentially not a soul kept tabs on them.

10   Then there are judges who are **overly** lenient because... well, they just choose to be. In February 2002, a New Mexico woman with two prior DUI convictions was driving drunk when she swerved into an oncoming car, killing a 35-year-old man (also **inebriated**). Yet a judge sentenced her to just 30 days in jail, a decision that the **enraged** prosecutor called "a joke." Not many years ago in Maryland, a man who caused an accident that killed a woman got off with a $500 fine, three years' probation and community service. Noting the offender's injuries, the judge said, "You've punished yourself," and soon after let the man leave town for a bowling tournament.

11   With so much shielding drunk drivers, it's tough to come up with solutions. But Maine may be onto something. After a first conviction in that state, drunk drivers lose their license for at least 90 days, then get a "conditional" license. If during the next 12 months they're stopped with any alcohol in their system, they lose their license for a full year. Mothers Against Drunk Driving wants other states to adopt similar standards.

12   __E__. And when it comes to repeat offenders, we have to do the most commonsense thing of all: take away their keys. Maybe forever.

(Words: 893)

• Second Reading •

Directions: Read the text again more carefully to find enough information for Exercises I, II, III, IV & V.

Exercise I Understanding Text Organization

Directions: You may find there are a few sentences (segments) missing from the passage. Read the article through and decide where the following sentences should go.

1. All those smashed drivers aren't just playing Russian roulette with their own lives.
2. Almost one-fifth of the guilty drivers got unsupervised probation.

3. No drunk-driving death is easy to take, but this one had a sickening twist.
4. Of course we have to both toughen laws and then be willing to throw the book at drunk drivers.
5. All her dreams ended when a pickup truck slammed into her Toyota Tercel at 60 miles per hour.

Exercise II Multiple-Choice Questions

Directions: Please choose the best answer from the four choices given.

1. Romero reportedly tested _____ the state's legal blood-alcohol limit.
   A. within
   B. a little over
   C. at more than double
   D. three times
2. According to the writer's research, _____ drunk-driver arrests in this country involve repeat offenders.
   A. 4,000
   B. 5,000
   C. 500,000
   D. 400,000
3. By _____ law, the drunk drivers will be given back their licenses after a year.
   A. state
   B. constitution
   C. federal
   D. criminal
4. In 2001, drunk drivers killed over 5,000 innocent people—almost _____ the toll of the 9/11 terror attacks that year.
   A. the same
   B. twice
   C. three times
   D. four times
5. In _____, drunk drivers will lose their license for at least 90 days after the first conviction drunk driving.
   A. Maryland

B. Massachusetts

C. Maine

D. Montgomery

Exercise III   Word Matching

Directions: Please choose from among the supplied words to explain the original forms of the boldfaced words in the following sentences.

A. causalities   B. lenient   C. narrowly escape   D. huge   E. irritating

1. It turned out that Romero had been arrested for drunk driving a **whopping** six times before.
2. It turns out that lenient judges and kid-glove laws allowed Romero to **slip through the cracks**.
3. Most **infuriating** of all, Romero's story is far from unusual.
4. In 2001, drunk drivers killed over 5,000 innocent people—almost double the **toll** of the 9/11 terror attacks that year.
5. It's become a national disgrace for several reasons, but **lax** laws are among the biggest.

Exercise IV   Short-Answer Questions

Directions: Please answer the following questions briefly in your own words.

1. Was Romero drunk or sober when his pickup crashed into Sonja De Vries's Toyota Tercel?
2. How many drunk-driver arrests in America involve repeat offenders?
3. Which state in America does best in dealing with drunk-driver offenses?

Exercise IV   Discussion

Directions: Please discuss the following questions in pairs or groups.

1. What do you think is the main cause of traffic accidents?
2. What should people do to avoid such tragic traffic accidents?

Text C

Expel These Teachers

By Michael Crowley

1   New York City public school teacher Wayne Brightly did not belong in a classroom. He was the kind of guy New York State had in mind when it decreed that all its teachers had to pass certification tests by 2003. These would measure the instructors' basic skills in English, reading and math, their understanding of teaching techniques, and their expertise in the subject they teach. You might say that when put to the test, Brightly did dumbly. He flunked twice, which got him nervous. So the middle school teacher reportedly had his old friend Rubin Leitner use a fake ID and take the test for him. Even though Leitner was no Einstein himself—he has a history of mental problems and had once been homeless—he scored far better on the test than Brightly ever did. The sudden improvement was enough to draw the suspicion of state officials, who uncovered the scam. Brightly was reassigned to an administrative job while Schools Chancellor Joel Klein sparred with the teachers union over efforts to get Brightly fired quickly. But the scary thing is that Brightly had been teaching New York kids for 13 years.

2   Though most of America's teachers are hard-working and capable professionals, some education experts say there are far too many unfit teachers like Wayne Brightly in our schools. Mary Jo McGrath, a California education law attorney, says school administrators consistently estimate that up to five percent of teachers are so bad they're "doing damage to their students."

3   "It's a serious national problem," says Abigail Thernstrom, a member of the Massachusetts Board of Education and an outspoken advocate of education reform. Too many teachers, she says, "are not up to the job."

4   The fact is, thousands of teachers around the country have repeatedly flunked basic certification tests. Yet because of powerful teachers unions, as well as understaffed schools desperate to hang on to faculty, many of these dullards continue to teach.

5   In Florida, an investigation by the Sarasota Herald-Tribune found that a third of the state's teachers, teacher's aides and substitutes had failed certification tests at least once. Nearly 1,400 teachers failed tests 10 times or more. One Miami-area language arts teacher flunked more than 40 tests.

6   In Chicago, an investigation in 2001 by the Sun-Times showed that more than 800 Illinois

teachers failed the state's basic skills test over a 13-year period. In the previous year, one in seven Chicago teachers had certificates that temporarily or indefinitely waived competence tests.

7   In Pennsylvania, nearly a quarter of the state's public school teachers struck out on their certification tests in 2003.

8   It's not like any of these tests are killers. Sample questions from Chicago involve simple grammar and math. One asked teachers to choose whether one day's storms were "worse," "worser," "worst," or "worsest" than another's. A question from Pennsylvania asks teachers to compare four sales commissions—one percent of $1,000 versus ten percent of $200, and so on—and pick the largest. A grammar question asks whether you would rewrite the sentence "Martin Luther King, Jr., spoke out passionately for the poor of all races," providing choices like "spoke out passionate" and "did spoke out passionately."

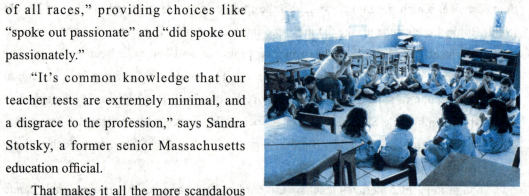

9   "It's common knowledge that our teacher tests are extremely minimal, and a disgrace to the profession," says Sandra Stotsky, a former senior Massachusetts education official.

10   That makes it all the more scandalous that states aren't getting tough with teachers who whiff these tests. In Pennsylvania, for instance, administrators responded to the mass failures by stressing other factors, such as teacher ratings. (Not that it always helps to have broader criteria: In New York City, where teachers are rated in areas such as classroom management and community participation, there was a 46 percent leap this year in the number of teachers who got failing grades from their principals.)

11   A few years ago, a newspaper in New York printed quotes from student-evaluation reports written by public school teachers. One said that a student "does not take to many things serious," and another had a "studdering" problem. One teacher wondered about a boy, "Why is he not learning or learning so but so little. How comes his past teachers have been passing him from grade to grade without he advancing or progressing academically. I will like to know what is causing the mental blockage." You think it might have to do with his teachers?

12   Yet getting rid of the bad ones means battling teachers unions that ferociously defend the lifetime tenure that many instructors get even at a young age. "It is notoriously impossible to

get rid of a teacher. I think more people are put on death row than lose their tenure as teachers through the legal process," says Philip K. Howard, a reformist who currently chairs the bipartisan group Common Good.

13   According to Howard, in a five-year period in the 1990s, just 62 of California's 220,000 tenured teachers were dismissed. And Time magazine has reported that only 44 of 100,000 tenured Illinois teachers were canned in a seven-year period. Even if only one or two percent of teachers are truly incompetent—well under the five percent that McGrath claims—those numbers should be in the thousands.

14   Firing a teacher can take years and cost the taxpayers plenty. New York City teacher Elihu McMahon was accused of making racially and sexually offensive remarks over a 15-year span. During 12 of those years, he was kept out of the classroom, yet McMahon still earned $700,000 in salary. He was finally fired in 2004.

15   One California school district spent $312,000 on legal fees to get rid of a single teacher. And when a teacher in the Jacksonville, Florida, area allegedly threw books at her students and claimed that evil spirits had invaded her students' eyes, it took a three-year process of evaluations and bureaucratic wrangling before her teaching license was revoked. No word on the expense of her case, but in general "a professional incompetence case is going to cost you from $200,000 to half a million," says McGrath, who has handled dozens of such cases.

16   Rather than fight to fire teachers, then, some principals prefer just to transfer them into some other unsuspecting school. Sol Stern, an education reformer at the Manhattan Institute, calls this "a game of passing the lemons."

17   The good news is that this problem has become a hot political issue. In 2001, Congress passed the No Child Left Behind Act, which set the goal of a highly qualified teacher in every classroom by 2006. That's only a target, but what's important is that the law provides an incentive for states to test their teachers. In the past, some school officials have insisted that test results remain secret on "privacy" grounds. But now, at a bare minimum, they'll have to report publicly on their efforts to boost the quality of teaching.

18   "There will be sunshine. And that will give people an opportunity, armed with information, to do something about it," says Chester Finn, a senior fellow at the Hoover Institution. With luck, that will hasten the day when no child is taught by a Wayne Brightly.

(Words: 1188)

Exercise I Discussion

Directions: Please discuss the following questions in pairs or groups.

1. Do you think there are many such Wayne Brightlys in China?
2. What do you think of China's present primary educational system?
3. What is an ideal teacher in your mind?

Exercise II Writing

Directions: In this unit, we've seen some aspects of the American society. In your opinion, which case is the most outrageous? Write a composition on your chosen topic in about 150 words.

GLOSSARY

A

abandon	v.	to withdraw one's support or help from, especially in spite of duty, allegiance, or responsibility; desert 放弃，抛弃
absolutism	n.	a political theory holding that all power should be vested in one ruler or other authority; a form of government in which all power is vested in a single ruler or other authority; an absolute doctrine, principle, or standard 绝对主义，专制主义
academy	n.	society of distinguished scholars 学会
accommodate	v.	to provide accommodation 容纳
accomplishment	n.	sth completed successfully 成就
acquaint oneself with	v. phr.	get familiar with 搞熟关系
acquisitive	adj.	greedy, avid 贪婪的
acquit	v.	to free or clear from a charge or accusation 无罪释放
affluent	adj.	rich, well-off 富足的，富裕的
affordable	adj.	that can be afforded 可以承受的，可以（买）得起的
aftermath	n.	a consequence, especially of a disaster or misfortune 严重后果
anecdotal	adj.	based on casual observations or indications rather than rigorous or scientific analysis 据粗略的观察，传言的
anesthetic	n.	a substance that causes lack of feeling or awareness; a general anesthetic puts the person to sleep 麻醉剂
approachable	adj.	friendly and easy to talk to 平易近人的
arcane	adj.	secret and known or understood by only a few people 神秘的，不可思议的
archetypal	adj.	archetypical, typical, classic 典型的
arrears	n.	money that you owe sb because you have not made regular payments at the correct time 逾期欠款
assertive	adj.	confident and direct in dealing with others 自信的
auction	n.	a public sale in which property or items of merchandise are sold to the highest bidder 拍卖
austerity	n.	an austere habit or practice 苦行节制的习惯或实践
avenue	n.	a means of access or approach 途径

B

batty	*adj.*	mad, eccentric 疯狂的，古怪的
belligerent	*adj.*	aggressive, confrontational 敌对的
best	*v.*	to defeat someone 打败某人
blatant	*adj.*	obvious, unconcealed 明显的，毫不掩饰的
bonkers	*adj.*	crazy 疯狂的
boor	*n.*	a person with rude, clumsy manners and little refinement 没有教养举止粗俗的人
boost	*v.*	to increase or improve something 提高
boot	*n.*	(*slang*) an unceremonious dismissal, as from a job. Used with the boot 撵走
Braille	*n.*	The braille system is a method that is widely used by blind people to read and write. Braille was devised in 1821 by Louis Braille, a Frenchman 盲文
brawling	*adj.*	making a noisy quarrel or fight 大吵大闹的
buddy	*n.*	a good friend; a comrade 好友，哥们儿
buffer	*n.*	a person or thing that lessens shock or protects from damaging impact, circumstances, etc. 缓冲
bust	*n.*	a situation in which the police go into a place in order to catch people doing something illegal 搜捕
by all means	*phr.*	(*fml*) yes, of course, certainly 一定

C

cajole	*v.*	gradually persuade sb to do sth by being nice to them, or making promises to them 哄劝某人做某事
Cajun	*n.*	one from Louisiana in the US who has French-Canadian ancestors（祖先从阿卡迪亚迁移来的）法裔路易斯安那州人
Caucasian	*n.*	anything from the Caucasus region; peoples of the Caucasus, humans from the Caucasus region; languages of the Caucasus; languages spoken in the Caucasus region 高加索人，白人；高加索语言
cavernous	*adj.*	resembling a cavern, as in depth, vastness, or effect 在深度、广度或效果上类似洞穴的；瓮音的，瓮声瓮气
channel	*v.*	direct, guide 引向
chip in	*v. phr.*	Each gives a small amount of money so that they can do sth together 凑钱，凑份子
chop	*v.*	cut, hack, fell 砍伐
cleavage	*n.*	the space between a woman's breasts, as revealed by a low-cut dress 乳沟

comes with the territory	*phr.*	"Comes with the territory" is a phrase. It means that something is included with something else. The phrase originated from sales. A salesman would be assigned an area in which he would sell his products. That area would be called a "territory." Anything that would be included with the assignment of that territory (such as an office or a car) would be said to "come with the territory."
comfort zone	*n. phr.*	One's *comfort zone* refers to the set of environments and behaviors with which one is comfortable, without creating a sense of risk. A person's personality can be described by his or her comfort zones. Highly successful persons may routinely step outside their comfort zones, to accomplish what they wish. A comfort zone is a type of mental conditioning that causes a person to create and operate mental boundaries that are not real. Such boundaries create an unfounded sense of security. Like inertia, a person who has established a comfort zone in a particular axis of his or her life, will tend to stay within that zone without stepping outside of it. To step outside a person's comfort zone, they must experiment with new and different behaviors, and then experience the new and different responses that then occur within his environment. [心理学]舒适区
commission	*n.*	appoint, authorize 委任
compulsory	*adj.*	obligatory; required 强制的
concession	*n.*	a grant of land or property especially by a government in return for services or for a particular use 政府为某目的将土地使用权有条件地转让
condominium	*n.*	one apartment in a building with several apartments, each of which is owned by the people living in it 一套公寓房间，一个住宅单元
connotation	*n.*	to suggest or imply in addition to literal meaning 含义
consign	*v.*	hand over, give up 移交，交付
contrarian	*n.*	one who takes a contrary view or action, especially an investor who makes decisions that contradict prevailing wisdom, as in buying securities that are unpopular at the time 唱反调的人，唱对台戏的人
cornerstone	*n.*	the fundamental assumptions from which something is begun or developed or calculated or explained 基石
cosmetics	*n.*	a preparation, such as powder or a skin cream, designed to beautify the body by direct application 化妆品
creaky	*adj.*	something such as a door, floor, or bed that is creaky creaks when you open it, walk on it, sit on it etc, especially because it is old and not in good condition 吱嘎作响的
crotchety	*adj.*	easily annoyed or made slightly angry, grumpy 容易恼怒的
crummy	*adj.*	of bad quality or unpleasant 劣质的，糟糕的
cushy	*adj.*	a cushy job or life is very easy and does not need much effort 容易而赚

钱的（工作）

D

daft	adj.	silly 傻
decrepit	adj.	weakened or worn out by age 衰老的，老朽的
deforestation	n.	It refers to the loss of forests due to overcutting of trees. One consequence of deforestation is soil erosion, which results in the loss of protective soil cover and the water-holding capacity of the soil 森林采伐
degradation	n.	a decline to a lower condition, quality, or level 退化
derision	n.	mockery, ridicule 嘲弄
dig up	v. phr.	to find hidden or forgotten information by careful searching 挖掘信息
digs	n.	lodging 宿舍
disclaimer	n.	a statement denying responsibility for or knowledge of sth 免责声明
downer	n.	one that depresses, such as an experience or person 使沮丧的事或不争气的人
dupe	v.	to trick or deceive someone 欺骗，愚弄

E

eligible	adj.	qualified or entitled to be chosen 有资格的
enraged	adj.	very angry 恼火的
esophagus	n.	the tube that connects the pharynx (throat) with the stomach 食道
espouse	v.	to give one's loyalty or support to (a cause, for example); adopt 拥护
extracurricular	adj.	outside the regular course 课外的

F

fabric	n.	structure, framework 结构
feat	n.	a specialized skill; a knack 本事
felony	n.	a serious crime such as murder 重罪
ferry	v.	to transport (people, vehicles, or goods) by boat across a body of water 摆渡
fiasco	n.	an event that is completely unsuccessful, in a way that is very embarrassing or disappointing 惨败
flaunt	v.	show off, 显摆，炫耀
flock	n.	gather, move together in great numbers 成群结队
footage	n.	film that has been shot 片子（原义是电影胶片）
fraternity	n.	a chiefly social organization of men students at a college or university, usually designated by Greek letters 男大学生组织，男生会

fret	v.	worry, vex 着急，不安
frustrating	adj.	preventing realization or attainment of a desire 令人沮丧的

G

gerontology	n.	the scientific study of old age and its effects on the body 老年病学
goggles	n. pl.	Goggles or safety glasses are forms of protective eyewear that usually enclose or protect the eye area in order to prevent particulates, water or chemicals 护目镜

H

harrowing	adj.	extremely distressing; agonizing 令人极其痛苦的，极其苦恼的
hold true	v. phr.	(colloq) be true 是真实的
hone	v.	to sharpen, to groom 打磨，磨炼
horrendous	adj.	awful, terrible 可怕的
hospice	n.	a program of medical and emotional care for the terminally ill 收容所
huddle	v.	crowd together 挤到一块儿
Hurricane Katrina	n.	occurring in 2005, it was the costliest hurricane of the Atlantic hurricane season, as well as one of the five deadliest, in the history of the United States 飓风卡特里娜
hygienist	n.	one who helps a dentist by cleaning patients' teeth and giving advice about keeping teeth healthy 保健专家

I

icky	adj.	distasteful 没有品位的
impending	adj.	upcoming（危险）临头的，即将发生的
inadequacy	n.	a weakness or failing 弱点，不足
inebriated	adj.	drunk 醉酒
infatuation	n.	a foolish, unreasoning, or extravagant passion or attraction 沉迷
infuriating	adj.	extremely furious 令人十分恼怒
internship	n.	a student or a recent graduate undergoing supervised practical training 实习，见习
inundation	n.	flooding, by the rise and spread of water, of a land surface that is not normally submerged（水）淹没
irascible	adj.	hot-tempered 脾气暴躁的

J

jab	v.	to stab or pierce 刺入或刺穿
jibe with	v. phr.	to agree with 符合
juggle	v.	to keep (more than two activities, for example) in motion or progress at one time 许多事情都兼顾

K

keep sth in perspective	v. phr.	to keep sth in a way that doesn't exaggerate any aspect 正确看待问题
kid–glove	adj.	a way of treating someone kindly and carefully because they easily become upset 和蔼而小心的

L

laid–back	adj.	(*infml*) Having a relaxed or casual atmosphere or character; easygoing 休闲的，悠然的
largesse	n.	(*fml*) when one gives money or gifts to people who have less than they do, or the money or gifts that they give 慷慨大方
legacy	n.	sth handed down from an ancestor or a predecessor or from the past 遗产
levee	n.	an embankment raised to prevent a river from overflowing 护坡，堤
literal	adj.	factual 实际的
logger	n.	one who logs trees; a lumberjack 伐木工
lout	n.	a very rude and violent person 举止粗鲁的人

M

makeover	n.	an overall treatment to improve the appearance or change the image 整容，变脸
mammoth	adj.	extremely large 巨大的
mature	adj.	of, relating to, or characteristic of full development, either mental or physical 身心成熟的
median	n.	It is one type of average, found by arranging the values in order and then selecting the one in the middle. If the total number of values in the sample is even, then the median is the mean of the two middle numbers. The median is a useful number in cases where the distribution has very large extreme values which would otherwise skew the data 中项，中位数
misdemeanor	n.	a crime—less serious than a felony—which is punishable by fine or

		imprisonment in a city or county jail rather than in a penitentiary 轻罪
mutter	v.	grumble in an indistinct voice 咕哝着抱怨

N

nemesis	n.	an opponent that cannot be beaten or overcome 难以取胜的对手，劲敌，死对头
nostalgia	n.	a longing for the past, often in idealized form 怀旧
nuanced	adj.	showing a very slight difference in meaning, feeling, tone, or color 微妙的差异
nudge	v.	to push against gently, especially in order to gain attention or give a signal 提醒
numerology	n.	the study of the occult meanings of numbers and their supposed influence on human life. 数字命理学
nurture	v.	to help grow or develop; cultivate 培养
nuts	adj.	crazy 发狂的

O

obligation	n.	promise, duty or condition indicating what action should be taken 义务，职责，责任
obscene	adj.	extremely unfair, immoral, or unpleasant, especially in a way that makes you angry 猥亵的
omen	n.	a phenomenon supposed to portend good or evil; a prophetic sign 预兆
opaque	adj.	impenetrable by light; neither transparent nor translucent 不透明的
ornament	n.	decoration, embellishment 装饰物
outrank	v.	to take precedence or surpass others in rank 超过 (级别高于)
overflow	v.	to have a boundless supply; be superabundant 充满，洋溢
overly	adj.	to an excessive degree 过于

P

paddle	n.	a small wooden instrument used at an auction 竞拍牌
peatland	n.	The simple definition of a peatland is an area where peat is found. Peat, or turf as it is often called in Ireland, is a type of soil that contains a high proportion of dead organic matter, mainly plants, that has accumulated over thousands of years. Close inspection can reveal the types of plants that grew, died and accumulated to form a piece of peat. 泥炭地
peek	n.	peep, a secret look 偷窥
plasma	n.	It is a distinct phase of matter, separate from the traditional solids,

liquids, and gases. It is a collection of charged particles that respond strongly and collectively to electromagnetic fields, taking the form of gas-like clouds or ion beams. Since the particles in plasma are electrically charged (generally by being stripped of electrons), it is frequently described as an "ionized gas." 此处指 Digital High Definition Plasma TV 数字高清等离子电视

plead	v.	to appeal earnestly; to declare oneself to be (guilty or not guilty) in answer to a charge 表示服罪或不服罪
pleasantry	n.	things that you say to someone in order to be polite, but which are not very important 客套话，寒暄
pledge	n.	a solemn binding promise to do, give, or refrain from doing something 宣誓
pontoon	n.	one of several metal containers or boats that are fastened together to support a floating bridge 浮舟，浮码头
potent	adj.	exerting or capable of exerting strong influence 有影响力的
primarily	adv.	mainly 主要地
primp	v.	(old-fashioned) to make yourself look attractive by arranging your hair, putting on make-up etc. 梳洗打扮
probation	n.	a system that allows some criminals not to go to prison or to leave prison, if they behave well and see a probation officer regularly, for a particular period of time 缓刑
prodigious	adj.	huge 大量的，大批的
prompt	v.	to give rise to; inspire 引起
provision	n.	a condition in an agreement or law（法律）规定
pulp	v.	to reduce wood, paper and raqs to pulp to make paper 制成纸浆
put together	v. phr.	to construct; create 搞出来（一个活动等）

Q

querulous	adj.	complaining about things in an annoying way 爱抱怨的，爱发牢骚的

R

rebuke	v.	reprimand, reprove 责骂，责备
recalibrate	v.	to make correction once again; readjust 调整，使与……标准一致
reconciliation	n.	the reestablishing of cordial relations 和解
relieved	adj.	made easier to bear 松了口气的
resentment	n.	anger, bitterness, antipathy 愤怒，不满
respondent	n.	one who responds 回答者
runny	adj.	food that is runny is not as solid or thick as normal or as desired（食物

因未熟或变质而变得）软，粘，稀溜溜的

S

savvy	*adj.*	clever, knowledgeable 聪明的，有学识的
scandal	*n.*	a publicized incident that brings about disgrace or offends the moral sensibilities of society; Damage to reputation or character caused by public disclosure of immoral or grossly improper behavior; disgrace 丑闻
scrape by	*v. phr.*	have just enough money to live 勉强糊口
screw up	*v. phr.*	to make a bad mistake or do something very stupid 搞砸了
searing	*adj.*	extremely critical of something 尖刻的
seethe	*v.*	to be violently excited or agitated 大为光火
shanty	*n.*	a small rough hut 小破棚子
shenanigan	*n.*	bad behaviour that is not very serious, or slightly dishonest activities 恶作剧，诡计
shrimp	*n.*	any of various small, chiefly marine decapod crustaceans of the suborder Natantia, many species of which are edible, having a compressed or elongated body with a well-developed abdomen, long legs and antennae, and a long spine-like projection of the carapace 虾米
signature	*adj.*	typical 典型的
simulation	*n.*	operation in which a real situation is represented in another form 模拟
skeptic	*n.*	a person who habitually doubts generally accepted beliefs 怀疑者
slight	*v.*	to offend someone by treating them rudely or without respect 轻视，忽略
sloppy	*adj.*	not done carefully or thoroughly 草率的
slouch	*n.*	slump 弯的，弓的身子
snoop	*v.*	to try to find out about someone's private affairs by secretly looking in their house, examining their possessions etc 探听，打探
sorority	*n.*	a chiefly social organization of women students at a college or university, usually designated by Greek letters 女大学生组织，女生会
sour	*adj.*	If a relationship or plan turns or goes sour, it becomes less enjoyable, pleasant, or satisfactory 关系变坏
spasm	*n.*	a sudden, involuntary contraction of a muscle or group of muscles 痉挛，抽搐
spoke	*n.*	one of the rods or braces connecting the hub and rim of a wheel（自行车）辐条
sputter	*v.*	to make a succession of slight sharp snapping noises; crackle 噼啪声
standstill	*n.*	a situation in which there is no movement or activity at all 停滞，僵持
stealth	*n.*	avoiding detection by moving carefully 秘密，鬼祟
stingy	*adj.*	spending, using unwillingly 吝啬的，不大方的
stroll	*n.*	slow leisurely walk 散步，闲逛

stumble	v.	to miss one's step in walking or running; trip and almost fall; to proceed unsteadily or falteringly; flounder 踉跄
subside	v.	to sink to a lower or normal level 下沉
superstition	n.	a belief, practice, or rite irrationally maintained by ignorance of the laws of nature or by faith in magic or chance 迷信
surge	v.	to increase suddenly 猛增突然增加
surly	adj.	discourteous, rude 没有礼貌的
surplus	adj.	being more than or in excess of what is needed or required 剩余的
sustain	v.	maintain or continue for a period of time 维系，维持
swag	n.	an ornamental festoon 悬垂饰
swallow your pride	v. phr.	to do sth even though it is embarrassing for you, because you have no choice 别顾面子了
swath	n.	the space created by the swing of a scythe or the cut of a mowing machine 镰刀或割草机割过后留下的地方，此处借指砍伐树木后留下的一片片空地
swirl	v.	to move with a twisting or whirling motion 旋转

T

thereabouts	n.	near a particular time, place, number etc, but not exactly 大约，左右，上下
tinker	v.	to make small changes to something in order to repair it or make it work better 鼓捣
tolerance	n.	the quality of accepting other people's rights to their own opinions, beliefs, or actions 宽容
toll	n.	(fig.) sth paid, lost or suffered [喻]代价；牺牲
transition	n.	change, from one condition to another 变化，过渡
trump	v.	to outdo or surpass 胜过，超越

U

unbridled	adj.	unrestrained; uncontrolled 不受约束的
underpinnings	n.	a support or foundation (often used in the plural) 支持，基础
unnerving	adj.	frightening 令人感到恐惧的

V

vibes	n.	the good or bad feelings that a particular person, place, or situation seems to produce and that you react to 气氛，环境
vicious	adj.	severe or intense; fierce 凶猛，猛烈

volition	*n.*	the capability of conscious choice and decision and intention 自决，自主

W

whopping	*adj.*	very large of its kind 特大的，极大的

Y

yob	*n.*	(*Chiefly Br Slang*) a rowdy, aggressive, or violent young man [backward spelling of boy] 粗俗的青年